HEALTHCARE SUPPORT: A TEXTBOOK FOR HEALTHCARE ASSISTANTS

COLLEGE OF PROGRESSIVE EDUCATION

Edited by Imelda Duffy

CATION

Gill Education
Hume Avenue
Park West
Dublin 12
www.gilleducation.ie

Gill Education is an imprint of M.H.Gill & Co.

© Progressive Education Ltd 2008

978 07171 4512 6

Index compiled by Helen Litton
Design and print origination in Ireland by O'K Graphic Design, Dublin

A CIP catalogue record for this book is available from the British Library.

HEALTHCARE SUPPORT: A TEXTBOOK
FOR HEALTHCARE ASSISTANTS

This textbook is dedicated to the memory of
Anne Clinch RSCN, RGN, RCNT, DHA,
founder of the College of Progressive Education.
Her background was in clinical nurse education and she was visionary in
terms of the importance of education for care staff.

CONTENTS

ACKNOWLEDGMENTS   xi
LIST OF CONTRIBUTORS   xii
FOREWORD   xiv
INTRODUCTION   xvi

CHAPTER 1 – OVERVIEW   1
Background to Healthcare Assistants in Ireland   1
Types of Care Facilities   2
Community Healthcare Assistants   2
Funding for Home-care Packages   3
Overview of Chapters   4
FETAC Assignments   7

CHAPTER 2 – CARE SUPPORT   8
Introduction   8
Relating to Clients   8
Diversity Awareness   9
Partnership Approach to Caring   11
Client Confidentiality   16
Privacy / Dignity / Individuality   17
Advocacy   20
Care Needs   21
Human Growth and Development   22
Reflective Practice   27
Assignment Guidelines   31

CHAPTER 3 – CARE SKILLS   32
Introduction   32
Safe Environment   33
Communication   34
Breathing   35
Eating and Drinking   36
Elimination   37
Personal Hygiene and Dressing   39
Controlling Body Temperature   42

Mobilising	42
Work and Recreation	43
Expressing Sexuality	44
Sleep	45
Dying	45
Pressure-sore Prevention	46
Assignment Guidelines	49

CHAPTER 4 – SAFETY AND HEALTH AT WORK — 50

Introduction	50
Legislation Relating to Safety and Health in the Republic of Ireland	50
Safety Statements	51
Risk Assessment, Hazards and Risks	52
The Health and Safety Authority	53
Safe and Healthy Work Environments	53
Fire	55
Infection Control	57
First Aid	62
Manual Handling	64
Risk Factors in Relation to Health	66
Conclusion	67
Assignment Guidelines	68

CHAPTER 5 – COMMUNICATIONS — 69

Introduction	69
The Communication Process	69
Communication and Interpersonal Skills	70
Methods of Communication	71
Barriers to Effective Communication	75
Overcoming Communication Barriers	75
Therapeutic Communication	76
Learning to Communicate Effectively	78
Assignment Guidelines	79

CHAPTER 6 – WORK EXPERIENCE — 80

Introduction	80
Globalisation and Demographics	80
Employment Opportunities	81

Skills Audit 83
Work Experience 85
Setting Goals 85
Writing your CV and Application Forms 86
Interview Skills 91
Getting a Job 92
Employment and Equality Legislation in Ireland 92
Assignment Guidelines 94

CHAPTER 7 – CARE OF THE OLDER PERSON 96
Introduction 96
The Ageing Process 97
The Positive and Negative Effects that Ageing has on the Individual 100
The Benefits of Preparing for Retirement 100
Promotion of Healthy Ageing 101
Development of Positive Attitudes towards the Older Person 102
Needs of the Older Person when their Health is Compromised 103
The Role of the Healthcare Assistant 104
Promotion of Healthcare Issues in Care Settings 105
Needs of the Older Person with Chronic Illness 105
Needs of the Older Person with Cognitive Impairment and Physical Disabilities 107
Nutritional Needs Including Special Diets and Specific Needs of Older Residents 111
Care Settings and Services for the Older Person 113
Assignment Guidelines 114

CHAPTER 8 – CHALLENGING BEHAVIOUR MANAGEMENT 116
Introduction 116
What is Challenging Behaviour? 116
Causes of Challenging Behaviour 118
Risk Assessment and Risk Management 123
The Role of Staff in Reducing the Risk of Violence and Aggression 126
Creating Safer Environments 127
Communication 127
Identifying Challenging Behaviour at an Early Stage 128
The Legal and Professional Considerations Required in the
 Use of Physical Intervention 131
Assignment Guidelines 131

CHAPTER 9 – PALLIATIVE CARE SUPPORT — 133

Introduction 133
History and Definition of Palliative Care 135
How is Palliative Care Practised? 135
Where is Palliative Care Practised? 136
Palliative Care Team 137
Coping Skills for Patients and Families 139
The Role of the Healthcare Assistant 141
Communication Skills in Palliative Care 142
Management of Symptoms 143
Terminal Care 145
Last Offices 147
Cultural Considerations 148
Bereavement 148
Palliative Care for Children 149
Assignment Guidelines 150

CHAPTER 10 – CARE OF PEOPLE WITH MENTAL ILLNESS — 151

Introduction 151
What is Mental Health? 151
What is Mental Illness? 152
Causes and Treatment of Mental Illness 153
The Most Common Types of Mental Illness 154
The Mental Healthcare Team 158
The Role of the Healthcare Assistant 160
Holistic Care 160
Assignment Guidelines 161

REFERENCES — 163
INDEX — 171

ACKNOWLEDGMENTS

The production of this book would not have been possible without the input and resources of many people. The advice given by Geraldine McSweeney, Barbara Garrigan and Professor Margaret P. Treacy is gratefully acknowledged. The financial support given by the College of Progressive Education towards the production of this textbook is much appreciated. The project would not have come to fruition without this support.

LIST OF CONTRIBUTORS

Blathnaid Connolly BSc (Hons) RN CIDC Dip in Management RSCI Cert in Training and Continuing Education NUI ENB 998. Strong clinical and educational nursing background and involved in teaching and assessing NVQ (UK) and FETAC Level 5 Certificate in Healthcare Support since 2005 in the public, private and voluntary healthcare sectors.

Anna Maria Doyle MSc (Nursing Ed) RNT RPN Higher Dip in Gerontological Nursing. Strong clinical background in care of the older person and involved in the education of student nurses and teaching and correcting FETAC Level 5 Certificate in Healthcare Support.

Imelda Duffy BNS (Hons) RNT RCNT RN RM. An experienced registered nurse tutor and involved in the teaching and assessment of FETAC Level 5 Certificate in Healthcare Support since 2002 in both the public and the private healthcare sectors. Imelda Duffy is editor of this book.

Vanessa Griffin-Heslin MSc BA (Hons) RNT RN. Registered nurse tutor and involved with teaching and assessing FETAC Level 5 Certificate in Healthcare Support since 2003 in both the public and private healthcare sectors.

Breda Hanrahan BNS (Hons) RNT RCNT RN. An experienced nurse educator who was responsible for the education of healthcare assistants for many years in the public healthcare sector. Teaching and assessing FETAC Level 5 Certificate in Healthcare Support modules since 2005.

Annette Kelly RN RM RPHN Dip in Management NUI Cert in Training and Continuing Education. Background in midwifery and public health nursing. Worked as a nurse health educator for many years. Teaching and assessing FETAC Level 5 Certificate in Healthcare Support modules since 2005.

Martha McGinn BSc (Professional Management of Aggression and Violence) BA (Hons) Dip in Social Science RNID Cert in Psych-dynamic Approach & People with Learning Disabilities. NUI Cert in Training and Continuing Education. Background in intellectual disability and involved in education across disciplines in the public, private and voluntary healthcare sectors for many years.

Mary Power MSc (Nursing) RNT RN RM Higher Dip in Healthcare Risk Management. An experienced registered nurse tutor and Nurse Practice Development Coordinator, and Senior Nursing Manager and Coordinator of Intensive Care Nursing in the public healthcare sector for many years. Teaching and correcting FETAC Level 5 Certificate in Healthcare Support modules since 2005.

Mary Vernon RN RM RNID RCNT RNT. An experienced registered nurse tutor who also held positions in senior nursing management. Teaching and correcting FETAC Level 5 Certificate in Healthcare Support modules since 2002 in both the public and private healthcare sectors.

FOREWORD

Hippocrates and Florence Nightingale were two of the most inspiring visionaries in the history of healthcare. They realised that training and education were essential for the development of high-quality skills. They also stressed that the application of these skills must be governed by the highest ethical and moral standards. Over time, the principles of practice expressed in the Hippocratic Oath have become the central core of high-quality healthcare delivery. Even today, Florence Nightingale's classical text, *Notes on Nursing – What it is and What it is Not*, is essential reading for all involved in the caring profession.

Healthcare nowadays has become increasingly complex and sophisticated. Today's patients benefit from advances in technology and skills unthought-of a generation ago. Despite these advances the core principles of caring and respect for the dignity of the person remain as important as ever.

Along with the increasing awareness of the rights of patients are the duties and responsibilities of those caring for them. This creates new pressures for healthcare workers. Today we are more sensitive to issues of individual accountability and more aware of personal responsibility for our actions.

In an area where technology and information are increasingly dominant, the need for patient confidentiality and absolute respect for human dignity remains central. Ensuring that a patient receives the best care that modern medicine has to offer in an environment that preserves all of a patient's rights, dignity and comforts is a daily challenge for us all.

This is why life-long learning and continuing personal and professional development are of central importance for all of us involved in healthcare. Ongoing education ensures that we remain open to new ideas while preserving the value of proven established best practice.

We have become critically aware that no worker should be expected to undertake a task until he or she has acquired the relevant competence and all the necessary skills to complete an assignment. This puts an increasing responsibility on the employer and the employee; hence the growth of in-service training and professional development courses which have become central to the delivery of quality patient care.

In Ireland, the government has recognised the central importance of life-long learning and has established the National Qualifications Framework to oversee and monitor the development of high-quality educational and training programmes.

The framework provides for a single national and internationally accepted entity through which all learning achievements may be measured and related to one another. The framework facilitates access, transfer and progression to higher levels of learning across the education and training sectors.

At present there are ten award levels. Levels one to six are overseen by FETAC (The Further Education and Training Awards Council). HETAC (Higher Education and Training Awards Council) makes awards which start at level six and go as far as a doctorate at level ten.

This common framework allows for cross recognition and portability of qualifications throughout the country. It also allows for the mutual recognition of qualifications by countries throughout Europe through the Copenhagen and Bologna agreements and the Europass system.

It is reassuring to a student who knows that once a course has a FETAC or HETAC imprimatur then it will be recognised throughout the EU, thus facilitating further qualifications, skill enhancement and life-long learning.

I'm delighted and greatly honoured to be asked to write the foreword to this book.

The book provides a central resource for modules leading to the FETAC Level 5 Certificate in Healthcare Support (DHSXX) and covers a broad spectrum of integrated training for healthcare staff.

Each chapter is written by an author with a special interest and expertise in their chosen area. All the authors are qualified clinical nurses and experienced lecturers in nursing studies, and their writing contains a deep knowledge and understanding of their chosen subject.

The collected chapters provide an excellent coverage of the skills and knowledge required by carers working in the clinical area and is valued reading for anyone in the caring profession.

J. Bernard Walsh
Consultant Physician and Clinical Professor
St James's Hospital and Trinity College Dublin

INTRODUCTION

Imelda Duffy

This textbook is written for healthcare assistants (HCAs) who are undertaking the FETAC Level 5 Certificate in Healthcare Support (DHSXX) and working in a variety of care situations/facilities throughout the country.

The idea for this book came about in 2005 when sourcing a text for the first group of healthcare assistants (HCAs) from the private care facilities who were undertaking the Further Education and Training Awards Council (FETAC) Level 5 Certificate in Healthcare Support. No text from an Irish perspective was available and a seed was planted about the possibility of writing a book. It is a book that HCAs can use as a reference when studying for the award. This idea lay dormant for some time, but at the beginning of 2007 the idea was discussed with a group of registered nurse tutors and nurses who had specialist qualifications in various disciplines. The seed germinated and has now come to full bloom.

The FETAC Level 5 award forms part of the National Framework of Qualifications in Ireland (www.nfq.ie).

There are 10 levels within the framework.

The FETAC National Council for Vocational Awards (NCVA) Level 5 Major Award will be awarded to a candidate who reaches the required standard in at least eight modules, five of which are vocational modules (including mandatory and elective modules), two general studies modules (one of which must be Communications) and one Work Experience module.

The Healthcare Support Award consists of eight FETAC Level 5 modules, and is the Department of Health and Children's recommended qualification for all HCAs. The FETAC Level 5 Certificate in Healthcare Support (DHSXX) has five vocational modules, two general studies modules, one of which must be Communications and one the Work Experience module. Three of the five vocational modules are mandatory and these are Care Skills, Care Support and Safety and Health at Work (www.fetac.ie/guide/DHSXX.htm). The three elective modules to complete the certificate can be chosen from a selection of modules that are the most suitable and relevant to the HCA's type of work or care area. Some of the elective modules can be chosen from the following FETAC Level 5 modules: Care of the Older Person, Care of People with Mental Illness, Team Working, Nutrition, Palliative Care Support, Operating Department Care Skills, Introduction to Nursing, Rehabilitation Support, Activities of Living Patient Care,

Challenging Behaviour Management, Intellectual Disability Studies, Maternity Care and Support, Anatomy and Physiology, Care Provision and Practice, Human Growth and Development, Infection Prevention and Control, and Legislative Procedures and Quality. All FETAC modules can be viewed on www.fetac.ie with the exception of any of the above elective modules, which are locally devised.

The FETAC Level 5 Certificate in Nursing Studies (DCHSN) and Community and Health Services (DCHSX) have different mandatory modules and can be undertaken as a means of applying for a place on an undergraduate honours nursing or midwifery degree programme once certain criteria are met. The modules that are mandatory for using any of the above three awards as a progression route into a nursing or midwifery degree programme are Anatomy and Physiology, Introduction to Nursing, Human Growth and Development or Biology. Candidates must obtain five distinctions, including distinctions in the above mandatory modules, in order to be able to apply for a place on a nursing degree programme in most of the higher education institutes in Ireland. The FETAC Level 5 award, once certain criteria are met, is seen as equivalent to the Leaving Certificate Examination entry route for standard code applicants to nursing/midwifery, using the Central Application Office (CAO) process. This route into nursing may allow candidates an opportunity to gain a place on a degree programme. Information on FETAC/NCVA Level 5 as a means of applying for a place on a nursing degree programme can be obtained from the CAO website, www.cao.ie. Information on nursing degree programmes can be obtained at www.nursingcareers.ie.

This book is specifically written for HCAs who are undertaking the FETAC Level 5 Certificate in Healthcare Support (DHSXX) and working in a variety of care settings in the public, private and voluntary care sectors. It can be used as a course textbook that will assist in giving background information to support the classes for each module. The book covers the three mandatory vocational modules, the Communication and the Work Experience modules for the FETAC Level 5 Certificate in Healthcare Support (DHSXX), and a selection of the elective modules that are seen as most relevant to the care areas in which the majority of HCAs work. Each of the authors has been directly involved with the teaching, correcting and support of HCAs undertaking the FETAC Certificate in Healthcare Support and all have in-depth knowledge of the modules from a healthcare perspective. The authors have ensured that overlap of topics in the various FETAC modules will be kept to a minimum in the text and guidance will be given where overlapping topics can be located.

Many of the experienced HCAs have a wealth of knowledge and skills gained from many years of care work and personal life experiences. These experiences will be utilised during the course and built upon to assist HCAs in preparing for the many new challenges in today's healthcare environment. The programme offers the HCAs the opportunity to participate fully in the multidisciplinary care team. The knowledge gained throughout the course will increase confidence and job satisfaction. It will also develop core skills and increase knowledge relevant to the HCA's work area. It is essential that HCAs have this training to equip them with the knowledge and skills to provide best-practice, person-centred care to all service users in a variety of care settings under the direction, guidance and supervision of the registered nurse/midwife.

Until 2000 the HCAs in the Irish health service had no formal training. Some hospitals and care facilities demonstrated their commitment to the education of their HCAs by providing in-service education and training programmes for them. Courses ranged from a structured 2–3 weeks of theory to individual study days delivered in a classroom setting. Course assignments were corrected by the health facility staff. While these courses were very beneficial, there was no consistency of topics or fixed length of training and there was no recognised body to accredit them externally. In response to this lack of structured training and increased demands on care staff, the Department of Health and Children (DOHC), together with the relevant stakeholders, introduced a training programme for HCAs. This programme consisted of FETAC Level 5 and accredited modules, some of which were developed specifically for the training of HCAs by relevant health educational personnel involved in the nursing profession.

Prior to 2000 the vast majority of HCAs in Ireland only received the mandatory moving, handling and fire training.

In the UK, as far back as 1972, 'training for HCAs as a matter of urgency' was mooted (Briggs Committee on Nursing). Since the 1990s the National Vocational Qualifications (NVQs) training is in place in the UK. In Ireland the Report on the Commission on Nursing, *A Blueprint for the Future* (DOHC, 1998), recommended the development of the HCA role. HCAs are now being offered the opportunity, for the first time, to gain a recognised FETAC Level 5 qualification that demonstrates their competencies and skills.

During 2000–2001 the FETAC Level 5 Certificate in Healthcare Support was run as a pilot programme in the public sector in fourteen sites throughout the country. Following evaluation of the pilot programme, courses commenced in all the major public hospitals in the autumn of 2002. They were held in the Centres for Nurse Education (previously the schools of nursing) and taught for the most part by registered nurse tutors. In 2005 a concerted effort to up-skill care assistants, known as the 'one step up' competency development programme, took place in the private care sector. HCAs undertaking the award work through a closely monitored and in-depth programme, which increases knowledge and builds on existing clinical skills. Competencies are assessed in both clinical skills and knowledge. Feedback from both new and experienced HCAs who have completed the certificate indicates the importance of gaining knowledge and increasing clinical skills. It is equally important that confidence, a sense of achievement and self-worth is achieved. The provision of training is perceived to have benefited the HCA both on a professional and personal level (McKenna *et al.*, 2003). It gives the HCA an opportunity to gain a recognised national qualification and the option of furthering his/her education and career. Views from managers in care on the benefits of the training of the HCAs were also seen as very positive (Keeney *et al.*, 2005).

While writing this book, new guidelines, *Draft National Quality Standards for Residential Care Settings for Older People*, were published in March 2007 (www.dohc.ie/publications). These standards were revised and republished for public consultation in July 2007. The *National Quality Standards for Residential Care Settings for Older People in Ireland* was published on 11 March 2008 (www.hiqa). Standard 24, Criteria 24.2 states, 'All newly recruited care staff and those in posts less than one year commence training to FETAC Level 5 or equivalent within two years of taking up employment. Long-standing care staff have their competency and skills assessed to determine their need for further training and suitable arrangements are put in place to meet their educational needs' (HIQA, 2008). The standards, when signed into law, will change the way residential care facilities in both the public and private sectors are inspected and regulated and more emphasis will be placed on the education and training of care staff. By the time this book is published, the standards should be signed into law. It is vital that all HCAs are given the opportunity to acquire the necessary knowledge, skills and competencies to understand the rationale underpinning care so that they can provide 'evidence-based person-centred care' under the direction and supervision of the registered nurse.

It is hoped that this textbook, written to support and underpin the FETAC Level 5 Certificate in Healthcare Support (DHSXX), will be an informative resource and valuable aid for all healthcare assistants studying for the FETAC Level 5 qualification.

OVERVIEW

Annette Kelly

Background to Healthcare Assistants in Ireland; Types of Care Facilities; Community Healthcare Assistants; Funding for Home-care Packages; Overview of Chapters; FETAC Assignments

Background to Healthcare Assistants in Ireland

The healthcare assistant (HCA) is a valued member of the multidisciplinary team who supports the delivery of patient/client care under the supervision and direction of the registered nurse. The HCA engages in both direct and indirect patient/client care. There are many titles associated with the role of the HCA working across the Irish health service, for example *ward attendant, care attendant, nurse's aide, hospital orderly, support worker, ward assistant* and *auxiliary*. Following the Commission on Nursing, one of the recommendations of the working group was the introduction of the HCA as a member of the healthcare team 'to assist and support the nursing and midwifery function' (DOHC, 1998). Recommendations were also made in relation to the education and training of the HCA. The healthcare assistant (HCA) is the title that is to be adopted across all healthcare settings. The National Health Strategy 'Quality and Fairness, Health System for You' (1998) stated that one of its initiatives was 'to introduce the grade of HCA as a member of the healthcare team to assist and support nurses and midwives' (1998).

Currently there is no statutory requirement in Ireland for the HCA to have completed any recognised training and this is a grave concern for many professionals because HCAs provide care for some of the most vulnerable people in society, i.e. older people and disabled. This situation is about to change with the publication of the *National Quality Standards for Residential Care Settings For Older People in Ireland* (2008). This textbook is coming at a very opportune time as most of the modules covered in the FETAC Level 5 Certificate in Healthcare Support touch on many aspects that the various standards outline.

The role of the HCA today is to support the delivery of patient/client care under the direction and supervision of the registered nurse (Shannon *et al.*, 2001). Nursing staff should only delegate duties to the HCA for which she/he has been trained. HCAs are accountable for their actions in providing care to clients/residents, but they must not take on work that they are not trained to provide. The report of the Working Group (DOHC, 2001) states, 'It is essential that healthcare assistants are accountable to the nurse/midwife, clients/patients and to their employer for performing all tasks and responsibilities, including those delegated to them, to the best of their ability' (DOHC, 2001). Duties allocated to the HCA will depend on the care setting, the client's needs and the reporting structure.

Types of Care Facilities

HCAs work in a variety of care facilities in the public, private and voluntary care sectors. The care facilities range from the acute general, maternity and children's hospitals, to the long-stay care facilities. Long-stay facilities can be hospitals and nursing homes that are public, voluntary or private. HCAs also work in the community, in day-care facilities, day hospitals and in the client's own home.

Community Healthcare Assistants

This is a relatively new position that has emerged in the last fifteen years. Until recently, a HCA working in the community was part of the Health Services Executive (HSE). The HCA working under the HSE is part of a team in the community, alongside the registered nurse and the public health nurse (PHN). The PHN has overall responsibility for ensuring that the nursing care needs of his/her area are carried out effectively. There are now many private home-care agencies employing HCAs to provide services to people regardless of age who wish to remain in their own home but need assistance with activities of daily living. Regardless of whether the HCA is working in the public or private sector in the community, many skills are involved. One of the most important things to remember is that as a HCA in the community you are a visitor in the client's home and may be asked to leave at any time. Confidentiality is of the utmost importance as HCAs in the community are placed in a position where they may be the confidant for the client and may hear very personal details of the client's business. HCAs providing care in the client's home can be somewhat isolated, so it is essential that all have a FETAC Level 5 qualification to be in a position to provide quality care. This certificate will assist the HCA to provide 'evidence-based, person-centred care' for all clients under the direction of the registered nurse. Regular updating is required to keep abreast of developments and ensure best practice is followed in all situations.

Funding for Home-care Packages

Most older people prefer to live independently and remain in their own home for as long as possible. In his keynote address at the AGM of Age Action Ireland, Professor Brendan Drumm (CEO, HSE) stated, 'Much greater attention must be given to community and home-care services … so that people could live longer in their own homes without having to go into residential care' (Age Action Ireland, 2007).

Investment of €110m was provided in 2006 and €40m in 2007 by the Minister of Health Mary Harney in the December 2005 budget for improvements in both home and community-based care support for older people. Part of this investment was to provide home-care packages to assist older people to remain in the comfort of their own home, where the majority want to be. The home-care packages are used to fund care services, depending on the client's needs. These packages include the services of nurses, healthcare assistants and many other professionals. By the end of 2007 it is estimated that a total of 2,000 additional home-care packages will provide assistance to older persons to allow them continue to live in their own homes. These packages are seen as a means of keeping older people out of the acute hospital system or long-term care facilities for as long as possible. The Home Care Support Scheme is operated by the HSE and its aim is to assist and support older people who wish to continue to live independently in their own homes but who may require some support to achieve this. The support required will be assessed at a local level, based on specific needs, and each support package will be tailored to the individual. In some parts of the country services are operated by the HSE and in other areas services are delivered by private agencies or voluntary organisations.

The next section provides a brief outline of each chapter. Nine FETAC Level 5 modules are covered in this book. The Healthcare Support Award consists of eight FETAC Level 5 modules. The FETAC Level 5 Certificate in Healthcare Support (DHSXX) has five vocational modules and two general studies modules, one of which must be Communications and the Work Experience module. Three of the five vocational modules are mandatory www.fetac.ie/guide/DHSXX.htm).

The book covers the three mandatory vocational modules, which are Care Skills, Care Support and Safety and Health at Work. It also covers Communications and the Work Experience modules. The elective modules that are seen as most relevant to the care areas in which the majority of HCAs work are covered in the book.

Learners will find a lot of information in the chapters that will assist them during their course and with the various assignments for the modules.

This book is intended as a resource for learners. It is not meant to be all-inclusive for each of the specific learning outcomes of the modules covered; rather it provides support to the taught course.

Overview of Chapters

CHAPTER 2

Core principles of care will be explored in Chapter 2. Dignity, respect, confidentiality, client independence and choice are basic core principles that all clients/residents are entitled to, regardless of the type of care facility they find themselves in. These core principles are essential in all care situations and this chapter is based on the FETAC Level 5 Module Support Care. Standard 4 in the *Draft National Quality Standards* deals with privacy and dignity and how these standards are respected and achieved. Standard 17 discusses autonomy and independence for all residents. Maintaining independence and having choice and control over one's life is essential, regardless of where the individual is living. This chapter will also examine the process of reflection and how reflection can be used as both a learning tool and as a means of self-improvement.

CHAPTER 3

Chapter 3 will follow the FETAC Level 5 Care Skills Module, which deals with basic care skills that clients/residents may need assistance with at various stages in their life cycle. This care may be required for people with disabilities, older people or people of any age who, for one reason or another, require assistance with activities of daily living. The role of the HCA in the prevention of pressure sores will also be discussed. This module has a very practical approach and basic care skills are taught in the classroom and practised in the clinical area. Assessment of clinical competence in specific care skills is undertaken by the registered nurse in the clinical field.

CHAPTER 4

The FETAC Level 5 Safety and Health at Work Module will be outlined in this chapter. This module is a generic module for many major FETAC awards. When it is taught as part of the FETAC Level 5 Certificate in Healthcare Support, greater emphasis will be put on specific aspects of safety and health relevant to the healthcare environment. The principles of infection control will be outlined, with emphasis on the prevention and control of cross-infection in all care facilities. Given the problems with MRSA and other infections in hospitals, nursing homes and the community, it is essential that updates on current 'best practice' in all aspects of infection control are provided for all care staff. Members of care staff are faced with many challenges in preventing the spread of infection. Every worker must take responsibility for their practice and must adhere to the correct protocols and procedures that are in place to reduce and minimise the risk of infections to clients/patients. Information on the correct disposal of clinical and non-clinical waste is required for all care staff. Hand hygiene is the single most important factor in the prevention of cross-infection and is seen as vital in the control of the spread of MRSA. All staff must be updated on a regular basis to ensure that correct procedures are being adhered too. This is crucial in today's healthcare environments where infection is causing great distress and pain to clients while at the same time increasing overall costs of care. It is essential that the HCA is fully informed and updated on his/her role and responsibilities in the prevention of the spread of infection. Standard 26 in the *National Quality Standards for Residential Settings for Older People in Ireland* deals with health and safety of the residents, staff and visitors. The issue of raising awareness on other aspects of health and safety issues in the care environment will also be covered. The responsibilities of the employee and employer under health and safety legislation will be discussed.

CHAPTER 5

Communication skills are essential in any environment and it is vital that all healthcare assistants practise good communication skills in all care situations. While most of the modules that make up the FETAC Level 5 Certificate in Healthcare Support cover aspects of communication, Chapter 5 is dedicated specifically to this FETAC module. The module is a generic module for most major FETAC awards, but, when taught as part of the FETAC Level 5 Certificate in Healthcare Support, greater emphasis will be given to equipping the HCA with the necessary skills to communicate effectively with clients/residents in the healthcare environment. The chapter explores therapeutic communication skills in meeting the needs of clients/residents with various communication deficits and difficulties. Communicating effectively and appropriately with the large range of disciplines that are involved in healthcare is essential for the smooth running of the service. The various methods and skills used to communicate effectively will be outlined.

CHAPTER 6

This chapter discusses the FETAC Level 5 Certificate in Work Experience Module and how it will assist HCAs to reflect on their work experience and use the knowledge gained in the course to improve their care work. Experiences from other work environments can be transferred to the care sector and this module will assist in identifying particular skills relevant to care. Guidelines for finding a job and preparation for interviews, are also outlined.

CHAPTER 7

Chapter 7 looks specifically at the FETAC Level 5 Certificate in Care of the Older Person Module. This module is essential for the majority of HCAs who work with older people, regardless of which care setting this may be in. The ageing process will be discussed and how it affects the various body systems. The specific needs of older people, depending on their care requirements, will be outlined. This period in life can be identified by failing health and loss of independence. Coping with illness, loneliness, loss of loved ones and a realisation of mortality are challenges that face the older person. Dealing with this stage of life depends on the extent of the emotional and physical support available and the ability of the older person's coping mechanisms which they have developed over the years. Demands for providing care for older people will increase with the projections outlined. This demand will occur in both the community and the residential care facilities. This module will assist HCAs to have a better understanding of the needs of the older person and how these needs can be met in an individualised, person-centred manner.

CHAPTER 8

The management of challenging behaviour is an ever-increasing issue in all care facilities. The *National Quality Standards for Residential Care Settings for Older People In Ireland* states, 'All staff have up-to-date knowledge and skills appropriate to their role, to enable them to manage and respond to behaviour that is challenging (Standard 21, Criteria 21.4, HIQA, 2008). Chapter 8 gives an overview of the FETAC Level 5 Challenging Behaviour Management Module (locally devised). This module has a very practical focus which deals with how best to manage challenging situations in care environments. It is a beneficial module for all care staff in order to impart the knowledge and skills that are needed to manage residents/clients whose behaviour is challenging, correctly and effectively.

CHAPTER 9

Chapter 9 looks at the FETAC Level 5 Palliative Care Support Module. Grief, loss and care of the dying person are discussed. These topics can be distressing for anyone, and HCAs need guidance and knowledge in their role in order to care for older people with dignity towards the end of life. Apart from providing physical care, the psychological needs of the dying also need to be addressed. There has been no suitable accredited course available to date for HCAs to meet these challenges and this module goes some way towards addressing this deficit.

CHAPTER 10

Mental health is a very important and relevant topic in today's demanding environment. The FETAC Level 5 Care of People with Mental Illness Module was developed to equip care staff with some basic knowledge and skills to be able to give care to clients under the direction and supervision of the registered nurse or the registered psychiatric nurse. An understanding of what mental health is and some of the mental illnesses that people can suffer from will be discussed in Chapter 10. Many clients/residents who need care due to medical conditions and/or advancing years may also suffer from various mental conditions. It is important for care staff to have a basic knowledge of these conditions as some residents' behaviour may be frightening to those who do not understand. Mental illness can be viewed by many as something to be ashamed of and some knowledge can help to remove this stigma.

FETAC Assignments

All FETAC Level 5 modules have a minimum of two assignments that learners have to complete to the required standard to achieve the minor or major award. The following is a list of assessment techniques that may be found in the various modules: Project, Skills Demonstration, Learner Record, Examination, Collection of Work and Assignments. Briefs with specific guidelines and detailed marking criteria will normally be provided by the tutor and/or the provider of the course. The briefs provide guidelines to assist the learner when preparing and writing the assignments. Clinical care skills are assessed and marked by the registered nurse in the workplace, while projects and other knowledge-based assessments are corrected by the course tutor. Assignments for one module can be utilised for another module once the criteria and marking schemes are matching. A brief outline of the assignments that are required for the modules covered in this book will be given at the end of each chapter.

CHAPTER TWO

CARE SUPPORT

Mary Power

Relating to Clients; Diversity Awareness; Partnership Approach to Caring; Client Confidentiality; Privacy/Dignity/Individuality; Advocacy; Care Needs; Human Growth and Development; Reflective Practice

Introduction

Human relationships are central and essential to the physical, emotional and sociological functioning of all people. Repeated surveys of the population asking them to name factors that they consider most important in their lives disclose that relationships figure predominately, and health features as a significant other factor. Therefore these two key factors are inextricably intertwined in relationship building between the caregiver and the care receiver.

Relating to Clients

The relationship that exists between a client and carer in many ways contains similarities to other personal relationships, and is one of an interpersonal nature. Gross (1987), who examined the subject, suggested that relationships 'needed to be rewarding', are 'influenced by degrees of compatibility between two people' and are built on the following:

- Trust: because it provides reliability, strength and confidence in the relationship.
- Honesty: because it provides sincerity and genuineness in the relationship.
- Other influences: including the amount of time the carer sees the person; the level of familiarity between the two people.
- When the client and carer share the same values, the client's self-esteem increases with acceptance and communication becomes easier because of the relaxed nature of the relationship.
- Clients and carers do not choose one another; the encounter is almost always coincidental. Hence it is important to establish what will promote a rewarding relationship.

- Core values of the client/carer relationship must demonstrate respect for the client's:
  - Ethnic origin
  - Values
  - Attitudes
  - Sexual orientation
  - Past learning
  - Religion
  - Opinions
  - Life experiences

This does not mean that the carer has to agree with everything the client may say or do. Nor does it mean that the client is expected always to be in agreement. It means recognising that the client has a right to have their own ideas and thoughts, and to have their individual integrity protected. The client must never be exploited, humiliated, ridiculed or taken advantage of, either physically, emotionally or financially.

Diversity Awareness

When caring for clients the emphasis is always on treating each client as an individual person with individual likes and dislikes. This is just as important, if not more so, when caring for people from different cultural backgrounds. It is essential to identify individual needs when meeting the client for the first time. If the client is unable to provide this information, perhaps a family member or companion can oblige. It is essential to gain as much background information for each individual client as possible. The carer must be familiarised with, and aware of, the cultural diversity of each individual when caring for people from a different cultural background.

When clients become dependent on others to provide their care needs, the emphasis must always be on treating each client as an individual person with habits and preferences of their own. This is paramount when caring for people from a different cultural/ethnic background. Consequently it is essential that a thorough assessment of each person is carried out on admission. This may not always be straightforward, as some clients may experience hearing, speech, comprehension or communication difficulties.

Areas where difficulties arise include:

COMMUNICATION

- Clients from different cultures may not speak English; therefore they will experience difficulty understanding and communicating. It must also be remembered that many clients may be unable to read or write in their native language. Gestures and facial expressions can mean different things in different cultures.

- Communication affects all aspects of care needs. A comprehensive assessment of the care needs of the client will provide sufficient information. Give the client a voice by allowing them to communicate and to make their own choice. Clients must be encouraged and given the opportunity to speak out, if possible, or make their views known, and the carer must make every effort to understand the client's needs. This method of approaching the client provides them with an opportunity to express their wishes and allows them to be autonomous in matters regarding their welfare.

- Autonomy can be defined as independence, allowing clients to make their own choices and providing them with the opportunity to remain independent for as long as possible. This must be encouraged as it fosters a client/carer relationship that enhances the quality of care and allows the client to remain independent/ autonomous. However, if the client is unable to communicate their wishes because, for example, of language or medical difficulties, always try to seek a relative or friend or an independent interpreter to translate and provide the necessary information.

RELIGIOUS VALUES

- Worship and prayer play an important part in the lives of religious people of all dominations. Many clients will have their own specific prayer and worship needs. Care staff must be aware of the client's religious needs and every effort must be made to try and accommodate their wishes in this regard.

DIETARY NEEDS

Many religions have special dietary needs (e.g. Roman Catholics fast on Good Friday; Hindu followers do not eat beef as the cow is considered the sacred animal). Other cultures have other requirements (e.g. food for Jewish people must be served in a sealed container and the cutlery must also be sealed and given to the client). Some clients prefer to have their relatives bring food to them. However, in many establishments this is not encouraged because it does not comply with infection-control regulations, in which case an explanation must be given to the client and their family.

FAMILY INVOLVEMENT

- In some cultures members of the community often make decisions on behalf of the client, or relatives may wish to participate in the care of the client. This must be remembered when planning client care. An example of this is that some clients prefer a relative, rather than the care staff, to assist them with personal hygiene requirements. This must be encouraged and facilitated whenever possible. Facilities should be provided for relatives of a client to remain within close proximity to the client if they so wish, particularly if a communication problem exists.

- Relatives will also have an involvement in decision-making, e.g. in some cultures females will not consent to treatment without their husbands' consent. On the other hand, members of other cultures may be offended if asked to contribute to their care planning as they may consider this to be the responsibility of the carers and healthcare staff in general.

- Some cultures have specific beliefs that may affect their care and may advocate the use of complementary therapies and homeopathic treatments. Clients should be encouraged to discuss these issues with the staff. Many of the complementary treatments are now looked upon favourably, including acupuncture and aromatherapy, and are sometimes used in the treatment of conditions among different cultures.

- There are many situations where the physical care of the client may differ because of the cultural needs, e.g. many Asian women do not like to bathe; they view this as sitting in dirty water and prefer to rinse themselves in clean water. Other cultures have specific skin and hair requirements, e.g. oils and gels to prevent their hair becoming matted and their skin becoming too dry and sore, a preference for many African women. Also, many women will not allow the opposite sex see them undress. Many Asian women will always cover their hair and legs. Sikh men always wear turbans and they are never removed in public.

- Each culture has specific requirements to care for the body following death. Some religions forbid the washing of the body, whereas some wish this procedure to be carried out by relatives. Other religions have specific rituals to be carried out by religious leaders following death. Consequently it is very important that all care staff are aware of the requirements following the death of a client from all cultural backgrounds. Most healthcare centres will have a policy in place to assist care staff in this regard. It is also important to have a record of the person to be notified following the death of a client. This is the responsibility of a member of the medical/nursing staff.

- Every client is an individual; the carer's role is the same for clients from all backgrounds, paying special attention to individual needs. Cultural differences may make a vulnerable person very anxious about unfamiliar carers and surroundings. Furthermore the client must not be judged because of their religious beliefs or customs; their beliefs and traditions must always be respected by the carers.

Partnership Approach to Caring

The manner in which a carer establishes and manages a relationship with a client can profoundly influence their recovery outcome. The carer has an opportunity to befriend and make a difference to the client by becoming an instrument of change; this is considered part of the therapeutic process of healing (McMahon & Isaacs, 1997).

The following approach will help to enhance the relationship:

1. Always explain clearly to the client what needs to be done and get the client's agreement before proceeding with any procedure.
2. Always respect the client's right to confidentiality, privacy and feelings of independence. Demonstrate respect for the client's life experiences and previous learning.
3. Assess the client's strengths and resources; thinking ability, flexibility and spirituality.
4. Always ensure that the relationship operates within the boundaries of the law.
5. Empower clients as much as possible to make their own decisions.
6. Allow the client the right to control his or her own environment.
7. Concentrate on the client's strengths; compliment them on their appearance.
8. Get to know the client's external resources; family and friends.
9. Identify other members of the caring team and support networks that can provide support to the client's advantage.
10. Develop a relationship that embraces comfort, maintains honesty, fosters trust and conveys an optimistic attitude.
11. Remember that personal growth continues throughout the life continuum.
12. Encourage clients to concentrate on the best aspects of their life, i.e. career, raising children, caring for aged parents, hobbies they pursued during their lifetime.
13. Demonstrate a sincere attitude and interest in the client's life history in the course of social interaction. This will add purpose and meaning to the person's life and assist in the journey towards recovery.

SOCIAL RELATIONSHIPS

A social relationship, incorporating companionship and friendship, is expected from all carers while participating in a therapeutic endeavour to assist in the client's recovery. Within a befriending, social relationship the carer helps the client to adapt to their situation, whatever it might be. A realistic perspective is gradually engendered within which the client is empowered, encouraged and renewed; any feelings of powerlessness and hopelessness are overcome (McMahon & Isaacs, 1997).

The presence of active listening in a friendly environment will give the client an opportunity to express feelings of anxiety, anger or disappointment. In a carer/client social relationship, clients will feel less isolated and any disturbances to the individual identity are given an opportunity to make a healthy adjustment.

Benefits of social relationships include improved social wellbeing and improved mental and physical health.

Good social relationships reduce feelings of depression, isolation, worry and anxiety, provide support for clients during difficult periods and enhance recovery from illness. Befriending, caring relationships help the client adapt to their situation (Forbes, 1994).

COPING WITH DIFFICULT CLIENTS

Many people may have experienced difficult relationships during their lifetime. Because of this they find it very difficult to trust people or even form close relationships, e.g. they may have lost a loved one, or been unsuccessful in their career or have been mistreated in another situation during their life experiences.

Past experiences of social breakdown in previous human relationships may result in feelings of worthlessness and demoralisation, and the client may perceive himself/herself as inadequate. These feelings are often expressed in the form of anger or panic attacks because of a fear of losing independence.

It is always prudent to remember that there may be a purpose to expressed aggression and hostility from a client. It may be a method of self-protection, or a way to keep control in a strange, uncertain environment. It could also be a response to stress and a means of self-preservation, protecting self-esteem and self-worth.

It is important not to stand in judgment and always remember to consider the fragility of the client in a vulnerable situation. Always try to look beyond the disease and the disability to find the real person.

POSITIVE APPROACH TO CARING FOR DIFFICULT CLIENTS

Always respond to clients in a positive way; never engage with others in disparaging discussions regarding the client's behaviour. Try to understand why the client is behaving in this way; try and put yourself in the client's position. Continue to act with warmth, empathy and genuineness and let the client know they are valued.

Never scold or underestimate the client's distress. The ultimate responsibility of the carer to the client remains the same as those to cooperative clients. The overall objective is to form a caring relationship with the client to reduce their feelings of anxiety and stress.

However, some clients may be unable to respond to the befriending relationship and the value of the relationship may never be known. They may feel uncomfortable and unable to trust self-disclosure.

PROMOTING WELLNESS

Using health promotion within the context of the caring relationship enables the client to feel physically and psychological good about themselves, irrespective of any disease process or decline due to illness.

The carer's relationship with the client can be used to facilitate this objective by promoting the following factors:

- The larger the network of relationships, the greater the feeling of wellbeing.
- Demonstrate concern for others.
- Demonstrate the ability to bounce back in adversity.
- Display courage in the face of life's difficulties.
- Provide a well-balanced nutritional diet.
- Encourage self-care and promote independence.
- Regular exercise: no matter how old the client is, a regular exercise programme will add quality of life by maximising residual function (Shephard, 1990).
- Carers can promote independence by encouraging the client to take self-responsibility by not restricting the client's opportunity whenever possible to self-care. Recognise the client's strengths and limitations and use them to promote a state of wellness, and support the client with praise and respect.
- Clients should be given the opportunity to continue with activities and to enjoy relationships of their own choice (Miller, 1991). The role the carer plays in the client's life is crucial to promoting wellness.

RELATIONSHIPS WITH VULNERABLE/CONFUSED CLIENTS

The carer is expected to maintain relationships with all clients, including those clients who have a decreased ability to engage in a relationship with the carer. However, this may not always be possible when the carer comes into contact with a client group whose dependency and fragility requires the carer to act with absolute integrity. This group includes clients who suffer from dementia, who are confused and disorientated.

This condition is mostly but not always seen in older members of the population. Scrutton (1998) looked at the subject of confusion in older people and estimated that between 5–10 per cent of older people suffer from confusion and the numbers are on the increase.

ASSESSMENT OF THE CONFUSED CLIENT

Mathieson *et al.* (1994) recommended that the carer should make an assessment of the confused client, whatever the cause. Client evaluation enables the carer to provide appropriate individualised care based on need.

Ascertaining client's recent behaviour includes:

- Have the changes occurred suddenly or gradually?
- What symptoms are being demonstrated by the client in the confused state that were not present before?
- Is the confusion more pronounced at any particular time or with a particular person?
- Is the client taking any new medication?
- What is the client's normal mental state? Check this with a relative, e.g. what is the client's normal level of clarity and content of verbal communication?
- Check the client's perception of reality, i.e. are they aware of their surroundings? Do they recognise their family members, the time of day, the year and the season?
- Check the client's ability to perform the activities of living (ALs), e.g. personal hygiene, continence/elimination care, eating and drinking and mobility. How dependent are they?
- Regardless of whether the client's confusion is temporary or progressive, the relationship between the carer and the client will have an impact on the client's confused state.

CARING FOR THE CONFUSED CLIENT

There are two aspects that must be considered when undertaking the appropriate management of the confused client. These include:

- The carer's approach and behaviour while carrying out a procedure.
- The carer's powers of observation.
- Always approach the client in a relaxed, organised manner. Never rush them or give too many instructions at one time, as this will exacerbate the client's confused state of mind. Never act in an alarmed way, as this will increase the client's distress; they will unconsciously think they have offended but not know why.
- The carer's behavioural approach to a confused client must be one that promotes a sense of quiet and calm. Focus on the client directly; maintain eye contact with a reassuring facial expression. Keep instructions to a minimum; clear and simple instructions that require either a 'yes' or 'no' response.
- Observation of the client's behaviour enables detection of any stress in the client's environment which may increase the client's confusion, e.g. they may not know where the toilet is located, which may cause incontinence and bewilderment for anxious clients in an unfamiliar environment.
- The main objective with confused clients must be an attempt to help the client maintain his/her optimum level of functioning. The carer should reinforce the client's function and purpose, re-orientate the client to their environment, and provide a structured, regular routine. Concentrate on the client's strengths and abilities. Allow

clients to self-care as much as possible, and try to empower them by engaging them in cognitive stimulation.

- Ensure a safe environment is maintained at all times. Examine the client's environment for any hazard that will harm their wellbeing and safety. Social interaction and reality orientation groups can be stimulating, using newspapers, radio and television. This can help clients to become socially involved and help to relieve the symptoms of both confusion and dementia.

Client Confidentiality

Personal information is valuable and enables the carer to care properly for the client. A complete history and background regarding details of the client's personal information is essential to carry out a comprehensive assessment of the client on admission to the care setting.

Personal information given in confidence by the client to the carer must not be communicated to others if this is the expressed wish of the client. For example, in the course of conversation during the daily routine, information given by a client in confidence or an incident that may cause embarrassment to the client must never be discussed with colleagues or other clients unless the health and safety of the client or other clients are at risk. This type of information is regarded as privileged and must only be passed on to the supervisor or colleagues if it is thought to affect the client's personal wellbeing or the wellbeing of others.

The client has a right to every consideration of his/her privacy concerning their care programme and treatment, which must always be treated as confidential and should be conducted discreetly. People not directly involved in the client's care must have permission from the client to be present during any discussions or consultations. All communications and records pertaining to the client's care should be treated as confidential and stored and filed securely. It is an offence to breach the confidentiality code with regard to client information.

CONFIDENTIALITY GUIDELINES

- Patient information must be discussed in appropriate places and with appropriate people (i.e. supervisor/manager) in private. It is unwise to discuss client information/condition while in the client's room, even if the client is unresponsive. They may still be able to hear everything that is said, which could cause the client unnecessary distress. Never discuss the client's condition outside of work, while off duty or while on coffee or lunch breaks with work colleagues.
- Communicate the client's personal information and concerns with your supervisor in private to avoid others overhearing.

- If asked by visitors or others to disclose information, learn to avoid inquiries tactfully and redirect to the proper authority, indicating that only the manager has the authority to disclose client information.
- Telephone inquiries regarding the client's condition must always be referred to the supervisor or the nurse in charge for direction to respond.
- Clients seeking information regarding their treatment or laboratory results must always be referred to the nurse or doctor or supervisor. Interpreting laboratory findings and evaluating a client's condition require a professional level of knowledge and judgment and this is outside the boundary of responsibilities of the carer's role.

Privacy/Dignity/Individuality

The most difficult aspect of the carer's relationship with a client is maintaining an appropriate level of intimacy. Maintaining an appropriate and successful relationship with a client depends on how the relationship is managed. When caring for a client it can be very easy to become over familiar, i.e. to treat the client in a child-like fashion, or indeed to become regimental in the approach to caregiving by ordering and expecting the client to obey. Clients must not be regarded as passive participants in their care.

Vulnerable clients exposed in this manner may experience depersonalisation and become depressed and withdrawn. They may consider this approach an invasion of privacy. Clients may be afraid to complain out of a fear of being labelled 'difficult' and 'awkward' and to avoid becoming unpopular with carers. Clients have a right to have their personal and private affairs kept confidential; to do otherwise is an invasion of privacy.

GUIDELINES FOR PROTECTING CLIENTS' PRIVACY

- Inform the client of what you are planning to do and get their agreement. This is called 'informed consent'.
- Protect the client from any unnecessary exposure of parts of their body.
- Always knock and ask permission before entering the client's room and secure the client's privacy before carrying out a procedure.
- Facilitate privacy for visitors.
- Never listen to telephone conversations.
- Never carry out a procedure against the client's wishes, but remember to report a refusal to your supervisor.
- Always listen and give the client the opportunity to express their preferences.

SENSITIVE PROCEDURES

The level of intimacy between a client and a carer will be influenced by the following aspects: age; sex; personality; ethnic origin; and educational/cultural background.

Scientific evidence has repeatedly demonstrated that women move more quickly into an intimate level of relationship than men. Men become suspicious or resentful where too great a level of intimacy is attempted too quickly. Therefore it is always prudent to develop a relationship slowly to avoid inadvertently comprising the client's rights to privacy and respect.

Our sense of dignity is influenced by many factors and can be based on past experiences, race, gender, culture, religion and social class. All humans have habits and peculiarities within themselves, which we would not want to share with the rest of the world. This is 'personal dignity'. Each person is surrounded by what is referred to as private space and will feel very uncomfortable if uninvited people invade that space. If a client feels that their private space is being invaded they will often react by just gazing ahead without speaking. Clients must always be treated with dignity and respect and the carer must remember to inform and explain and get the client's permission and agreement. Individuals are different and should be accepted as such by their carer.

Personal care invariably involves touch and particularly touching sensitive areas of the client's body. This can cause embarrassment or anger, and may be viewed by the client as an invasion of personal privacy and he/she may reject their dependence on others. Encourage the client to attend to their personal care needs for as long as possible. However, a large number of clients will be unable to self-care, in which case the client's personal needs must be carried out with dignity and respect by the carer in a discreet manner.

Society has unwritten rules about touch. These rules are different within individual families, different races and cultures. Always inform the client about the procedure, explain in simple terms that it may involve touching sensitive parts of their naked body and get the client's agreement or verbal consent before proceeding. Nakedness with other people in the room can cause embarrassment and place the client in a vulnerable situation.

Applying the following rules may help:
- Always secure privacy, i.e. close screens/ blinds.
- Keep as much as possible of the body covered during the procedure.
- Proceed with a relaxed approach, keeping the client informed of what you are doing.
- Address the client directly. Carry out a normal conversation and do not hurry or rush the procedure.

PROMOTING CLIENT SELF-ESTEEM

Self-esteem reflects the value that an individual places upon himself/herself, and it depends to a great extent on the way we are treated by others. Carers have an important role to play in promoting clients' self-esteem by helping them feel good about themselves, by valuing and respecting their individuality and encouraging them to become autonomous and involved in decisions regarding their welfare. A sense of being competent, autonomous and appreciated is basic to a good life experience, according to Davis *et al.* (1998).

The principle of promoting personal autonomy for clients underpins many of the guidelines for improving the quality of care in a range of healthcare settings (Wade & Sawyer, 1981). There is strong researched evidence to suggest that personal autonomy is of particular importance to clients in continuing care settings (Higgs *et al.*, 1992; Oleson *et al.*, 1994).

Despite the assertion by many clients that autonomy and independence are important to a good quality of life, carers working in healthcare settings frequently observe passivity and dependence among clients in their care (Barder *et al.*, 1994). This passivity contributes to dependent behaviour in clients by allowing the 'routine' to dominate care, and fosters an environment within which the client becomes a 'passive participant' in their care, which can lead to low self-esteem. A knowledge deficit of the carer and lack of experience provides this approach to care; this indicates the importance of continuous training and education for all care staff.

To avoid ritualistic practices, the following indicators help create a more client-friendly environment:

- Implement a system of care delivery that promotes comprehensive, individualised assessment and multidisciplinary care planning involving client participation. This system leads to a partnership approach to care, involving the client in the decision-making process and enabling them to remain autonomous. It respects clients' independence and protects self-esteem.
- Whenever possible, promote, encourage and facilitate attempts that encourage clients to participate in decisions about their care. Explain in simple terms any information concerning the client or arrange for a more professional opinion should the situation require it.
- Introduce patterns of communication that avoid exerting power and control over clients, i.e. always take time to listen to the client, provide as much information as possible to enable them to make an informed choice and offer support/advice.
- Modify the care environment, promoting independence and minimising risk, e.g. provide walking aids and mobile phones, encourage clients to keep in touch with friends and neighbours.
- Provide recreational activities and encourage the client to participate.

However, the situation is not always straightforward. For example, what of the client who is not independent or who, because of some disease or disability, is unable to make important choices about their lives? Clients may be unaware of their surroundings and unable to respond comprehensively; therefore they are unable to become involved or make any contribution. It then becomes a matter for the client's family, if available, and the multidisciplinary healthcare team to make a decision in the best interests of the client. Consequently others (the healthcare team) will make a final decision for the client, acting as their advocate in their best interests to protect their welfare.

The carer is a very important team player in this situation and is in a position to be the voice for the client within the decision-making healthcare team, e.g. perhaps the client expressed their wishes to the carer during their more lucid moments. The carer has a moral duty and responsibility to convey the client's expressed wishes to the healthcare team, thereby giving the client a voice and choice even though they may be unaware of what is actually happening. In this way the carer becomes an 'advocate' and acts on behalf of the client.

Advocacy

The word 'advocacy' has been linked to the legal profession for many years. When a solicitor represents and pleads on behalf of his/her client in a court of law, the solicitor becomes known as the client's 'advocate'.

Advocacy commences when a person represents the interests of another person. This requires complete loyalty of the person acting as advocate, who represents the wishes, needs and the interests of the client as if they were their own.

This usually happens because the person does not have the knowledge or skill to express his or her wishes. In more recent times the term advocate became a familiar term in the area of healthcare, where a qualified person represents the rights and wishes of a client who, due to illness or disability, is unable to make his/her wishes known.

Advocacy is defined as 'a process of acting for or on behalf of another person who is unable to do so for him/herself'.

DIFFERENT FORMS OF ADVOCACY

- *Self-advocacy*: speaking up for oneself, expressing personal needs and promoting personal interests.
- *Legal advocacy*: involves solicitors protecting their client's rights and interests in a court of law.
- *Citizen advocacy*: involves vulnerable people in the community who cannot achieve their needs, and some person of social standing in the community who may represent them.
- *Advocacy in care:* this process begins with the carer and the client both accepting that

their relationship is based on equality, trust and respect. The idea is to empower clients to help them to defend their rights, speak up for themselves and make their views and wishes known.

Generally the needs of people change as they age. They find themselves faced with complex issues, e.g. social welfare entitlements and medical cards. Many older people in the community are unaware of their entitlements and are unsure of how to go about claiming their full benefits. Therefore they need a trusted person to act as an advocate by giving them good advice.

In healthcare the client who cannot express their wishes may rely upon the carer with whom they have built a trusting relationship to express them. The objective therefore is to enable the client to be involved and have a choice in matters that concern their health and welfare. There are strong views to support the belief that the carer's role should be to help clients obtain the best care at all times, even if this means questioning the status quo, e.g. early-morning wakening times to accommodate the establishment.

Carers must focus on the ability to:

- Always act in the client's best interests.
- Provide friendship and emotional support to the client.
- Act as a mediator between the client and those providing services for him/her.
- Act as a guardian for the client's rights and protect from abuse.
- Preserve the client's values, dignity and self-respect and speak out on his/her behalf.
- Encourage the client to develop self-advocacy skills to enhance their ability to speak out and act on their own behalf.
- Observe local/institution policy on maintaining clients' records.
- Seek information to enable clients to make informed choices regarding their care.
- A greater part of client advocacy is the extent to which the carer succeeds in empowering clients so that they can actively identify their own needs, thus determining their future. This includes decisions about their health, welfare and the provision of care. However, this process may not always be straightforward because of complications associated with poor health or disability. Nevertheless the intention must always be to promote the benefits for the client.

Care Needs

Clients' total care needs may vary from person to person in intensity, but all members of society have similar fundamental human needs, referred to as 'the activities of living'. Activities of living are human needs, and some must be achieved on a daily basis. Generally a person will have the ability to attend to their own personal needs. However, when people become sick or disabled or are too young or too old, they are unable to attend to their own needs. This group of people are referred to as 'dependent', i.e. depending on others to carry out their daily activities (personal care needs).

When a normally independent person becomes dependent, the way in which these needs are expressed and fulfilled are different because of the changes associated with their environment and their illness. Moreover, basic human needs are the same regardless of how they are expressed and achieved, and the outcome is dependent on the individual's level of development or their state of health (Pulliam, 2001).

Human Growth and Development

Humans change as they age through the process of growth and development.

Growth includes: the changes that take place in the body, usually measured in height and weight and the amount of system maturity.

Development involves: the changes that take place socially, emotionally and psychologically. Development levels are expressed in behavioural and interpersonal skills.

People move from one level of development to the next. At each level they change in the way they look, think and act. Each level presents tasks that must be mastered before the person can move on to the next level. Tasks to be mastered are those that lead to a healthy and satisfactory participation in society (Pulliam, 2001). These tasks are defined by the needs of the individual and the expectations of society, and are achieved as the person progresses along the continuum of life stages.

Growth and development follow a pattern of basic principles of progression. This involves continuous movement from the simple to the more complex, e.g. baby sounds progress to words and eventually sentences.

Progression moves forward in an orderly way, but the rate of progression is individual to each person.

CONTINUUM OF LIFE STAGES

Birth to 1 month (Neonate)
The infant sleeps most of the twenty-four hours, awakes and cries to be feed.

Birth to 2 years (Infancy)
This is a time of rapid physical growth and development, e.g. the infant learns to sit up, crawl, stand and take the first steps. Other changes taking place during this period relate to emotional attachments which include parental and other family members. Alertness and increased activity are noticeable, teeth appear, there is a progression from milk to solid food and verbal skills begin to develop. The mother is the central figure of attachment. Growth and development progress are rapidly changing during this period.

Physical features of infancy: The head is disproportionately large in size compared to the body; the skin is thin and red in colour; there is very little, if any, hair on the head; and the eyes are dark blue. The head contains fontanelles anterior and posterior. These are soft spots situated on the front and the back of the infant skull. Conversion of cartilage to bone is not yet completed (this does not happen for 18 months to 2 years). Vision is blurred and the nervous system is not fully developed. Hearing and taste are also developed during this period.

Automatic reflexes developed at this stage of life include: Mono reflex (loud noises startle the infant); grasp reflex (touching the infant's palm causes the fingers to flex in a grasping motion); rooting (suckling) reflex (stroking the cheek causes the infant to turn his head towards the cheek in an effort to find the nipple to suck the breast milk). The infant is completely dependent on the care provider. The routine needs at this stage of life largely consist of sleeping, eating, elimination and hygiene.

At three months the infant has gained enough muscular coordination to hold up the head and shoulders. The infant can produce real tears, follow colourful objects with his/her eyes, and respond by smiling when stimulated.

At six months the infant can sit up for short periods and roll over; he/she can hold objects in both hands and direct them to the mouth; can respond to verbal sounds; cuts the first tooth; starts to eat more solid food; recognises family; and develops a fear of strangers.

At nine months the infant begins to crawl and may stand up if supported. More teeth arrive. The infant responds to her/his name and starts to say two syllable words, e.g. 'Mama' or 'Dada'.

At one year old the child understands simple commands, begins to take steps, eats table food and can hold her/his own cup.

Toddler stage (2–3 years)

This is a very active period and the main activities are investigating and exploring. This is also the time at which vocabulary and comprehension increases. The child learns to control elimination. He/she begins to become aware of the concept of right and wrong, can react with frustration to any attempts made to discipline and becomes more self-aware. The mother remains the main source of comfort and security. He/she will play with other children but will be very possessive in this period of development.

Reaching the end of this period, the child is able to walk and run, has the ability to feed independently and ride toys, and will begin to speak more clearly.

Preschool years (3–5 years)

Motor and verbal skills develop and the child becomes less reliant on the mother. The child begins to recognise its position as a member of the family unit. He/she develops rivalries with other siblings and forms a greater attachment to the father. Language skills are improved and the child asks many questions. At this stage, he/she becomes more socialised and cooperative and enjoys interaction with family members.

School-age children (5–12 years)
The child now has the ability to communicate, has developed motor skills and has started to learn how to write. The child also develops an increased sense of self, establishes relationships and builds on social behaviour through games, simple tasks and play. He/she chooses friends and begins to show concern for other living things, e.g. pets.

Preadolescence (12–14 years)
This is a period of great uncertainty and many children find this stage of development very difficult because they are on the threshold of great changes occurring in their bodies. Mood swings and feelings of frustration emerge. This is due to hormonal changes that arouse sexual characteristics and he/she may become more conscious of the opposite sex. This can be a period of stimulated growth where the limbs are disproportionate to the rest of the body.

Adolescence (14–20 years)
During this period of development individuals become sexually mature and begin to appreciate their own identity as male/female. Desires for independence and freedom are conflicted with the security of dependence, which can create personal turbulence for the individual. Personal coping skills and the ability to make independent judgments and decisions are also established during this period. Drawing conclusions, making comparisons and evaluating situations are also established. Decisions about the future career and/or education are also made.

Adulthood (20–50 years)
Independence and personal choices, choice of partner, establishment of career/home, family and children and choice of friends are formed during adulthood. Health is at its optimum during this period. Financial pressures are at their highest, which can cause stress for the individual.

Middle age (50–65 years)
Final stages of career and retirement. Children leave home to begin their own adulthood. Health can be at a very good level but some slowing down will be evidenced. This can be a very enjoyable period as there is more time for personal activities and leisure, but some may have responsibility for ageing parents.

Later maturity (65–75 years)

This stage is marked by a gradual loss of energy and a slowing down of activities. Physical changes emerge, e.g. sight and hearing weaken. Medical conditions may develop. This is the period of loss – of partner, friends and, to some degree, of independence and self-esteem – and it is a time for reflection on life experiences. Activities established in the previous periods provide support and social contacts, which is helpful. People in later maturity can function in a very positive manner and continue to make a valuable contribution to society.

Old age (75 years and beyond)

This period can be identified by failing health and loss of independence, dealing with illness, loneliness, loss of loved ones and a realisation of mortality. Dealing with this stage depends on the extent of emotional and physical support available and the ability of the older person's coping mechanisms developed over the years.

Fundamental human care needs

Development of skills and physical growth may vary from one person to another during life's continuum, but the fundamental needs are the same for all individuals. Human needs involve those activities that are requirements of all people to live their lives independently. The needs are the same for all people of all ages and they are the same whether the person is ill or well.

Abraham Maslow (1956) described a hierarchy into which he classified human needs using five levels – prioritising the most important – which has helped healthcare professionals to understand basic human needs and how people attempt to satisfy them.

First-level needs: physiological needs for food, water, air, sleep and sex.

Second-level needs: safety needs for security, stability, order, protection, freedom from fear and anxiety.

Third-level needs: psychological needs to be accepted and be cared for and loved.

Fourth-level needs: psychological needs to feel self-respect and to feel esteem from others.

Fifth-level needs: psychological need for actualisation through realising individual potential to its fullest.

According to the five levels described above, Maslow's hierarchy dealt with human needs, describing them as physiological, psychological and sociological. According to Maslow (1956) the physiological needs are top priority. Until these needs are satisfied it is not possible to move on to the next level.

Maslow's hierarchy of human needs was used to provide a structured approach to caring for dependent people. A modified version of this framework continues to be used by the caring professions to this very day.

In the 1970s and 1980s nursing researchers in the UK adapted Maslow's hierarchy of human needs. Further research of these structures continued and combined with the 'nursing process' at a later stage, which resulted in the introduction of 'A Model of Nursing based on a Model of Living', more commonly referred to as the Roper, Logan & Tierney (1980) Model of Nursing. The merging of the nursing process and a model of nursing introduced a systematic method of planning and delivering care to meet individual clients' total care needs.

Within this model of nursing, twelve activities of living were identified. These activities reflect the basic human needs that all humans must achieve and perform daily. Currently this framework of human activities is used to deliver care to individual clients when and for whatever reason they become dependent and require assistance to perform the 'activities of living' (ALs), which include the following:

1 **Maintaining a safe environment**: comfort, freedom from pain, avoiding injury and infection and monitoring change.

2 **Communicating**: verbally/non-verbally, forming relationships, expressing emotions, needs, fears and anxiety. Using smell, touch, taste, hearing, sight and sensitivity.

3 **Breathing**: meeting body oxygen requirements, maintaining a clear airway and lung expansion.

4 **Eating and drinking**: meeting nutritional needs, maintaining a healthy diet suitable to the individual.

5 **Elimination**: excretion of urine and faeces, maintaining normal function and control.

6 **Personal hygiene**: skin, hair, nails, mouth, teeth, eyes and ears. Selecting appropriate clothing, dressing and undressing.

7 **Maintaining normal body temperature**: physically adjusting personal clothing and body covers.

8 **Mobility**: exercising for health, maintaining muscle tone and circulation, counteracting the effects of immobility, relieving pressure to skin, changing position, using mobility aids.

9 **Recreation and play**: activity, pleasurable pastimes, achievement, independence and partnership in care/ rehabilitation.

10 **Sexuality**: expressing sexuality, fulfilling human needs.

11 **Sleep and rest**: adequate sleep and rest periods.

12 **Dying**: acceptance of inevitability, peaceful without pain or distress, needs met, needs to others met.

Within the 'activities of living' framework, the needs of the client can be identified, then client care planning and delivery are implemented to meet the needs of the whole person, generally referred to as the 'holistic concept of care'. This concept can be successfully implemented by knowledgeable, skilful and experienced carers. The above activities are discussed in greater detail in Chapter 3.

Reflective Practice

The process of reflection on practice is an active process of witnessing one's own experience, e.g. work experiences/practical tasks undertaken, in order to examine it more deeply. The purpose of reflection is concerned with implementing change in particular approaches to practice. This concept is not new (Kolb, 1984; Lewin, 1947). Its aim is to help practitioners obtain the maximum benefit from practice-based learning before, during or after it has occurred.

Reflection on personal work experiences is a process of deep thought. While looking back to a situation and during the process of caring for clients, there occurs a processing phase. This processing phase is the area of reflection: pondering over what happened during the event to examine one's own experience rather than just living it and projecting forward to the future, thinking about what could be done to improve the task the next time. This process involves both recall and reasoning according to Jarvis (1992). The ability to examine our own experiences and actions opens up the possibility of purposeful learning derived through practical experiences.

Reflection encompasses three identifiable stages:

- *The first stage* is characterised by an awareness of uncomfortable feelings and thoughts that the knowledge base is insufficient to explain current events: what happened during the task?
- *The second stage* is a critical-analysis situation, which focuses on feelings as well as knowledge: how did the carer and the client feel? How did the events affect them?
- *The third stage* is the conclusive stage, which involves the development of a new perspective for future tasks.

Good care practice involves the carer being mindful as they practise, i.e. thinking about what they are doing. This is more than being aware and taking action. It involves being actively alert to clues that the client is not coping or that they are finding the situation difficult. Such clues are identified through experience, i.e. working over a period of time with clients, experiencing similar situations. Expertise is developed through acknowledging patterns of behaviour and working with the client to address them (Benner & Tanner, 1987).

The concept of reflection can be refined by using the following terms: *reflection-in-action* and *reflection-on-action*.

- *Reflection-in-action* involves reflecting on behaviour as it happens in order to improve on the next action; in other words thinking about what is being done as it happens. Experience is gained through encounters with many different situations in practice over a period of time, providing the carer with the experience to make an automatic, informed judgment as the event takes place.

- *Reflection-on-action* can be described as a post-mortem, i.e. reviewing actions that have taken place and the knowledge that underpinned the action (Maryland & McSherry, 1997). According to Andrews, Gidman & Humphries (1988), reflecting on an experience is a highly skilled activity that requires the ability to analyse actions taken and make judgments regarding their effectiveness in particular care situations. Reflecting back on a situation allows the carer to formalise his/her thoughts and learn from them. This should take place as soon as possible following the event. Knowledge gained from delayed reflection may not be as rich or as accurate as the knowledge gained from reflection while performing the task, i.e. *reflection-in-action*.

Reflective framework

There are many frameworks to aid guided reflection. The most commonly used is the *reflective cycle*, first introduced by Gibbs (1988). This framework is very popular within undergraduate nurse educational programmes.

The Gibbs reflective cycle is a straightforward, practical application of reflection that provides guidance to the reflective practitioner.

Structured model of guided reflection

Description: describe the event. What happened?
Feelings: what are your thoughts and feeling about the situation?
Evaluation: what was good and bad about the situation?
Analysis: what sense could be made out of the situation?
Conclusion: what more could have been done?
Action plan: if the situation arose again, what should be done?
The Reflective Cycle (Gibbs, 1988).

Reflective scenario

The following hypothetical care scenario will help to provide a greater understanding of the Gibbs reflective framework and the way it can be used to improve practical procedures and help the carer to inform and improve future care procedures.

Attending to a client's personal hygiene

Description: Mary needed her personal hygiene attended to, which consisted of a morning shower carried out by two carers. Due to staff shortages on a particular day, care staff were unable to provide Mary's usual hygiene routine. Mary was informed that she would be given a bed bath some time in the afternoon. On the afternoon in question all preparations were made to carry out the procedure for the client. Immediately it became quite clear that Mary was not happy with this arrangement because Mary prefers to shower rather than be given a bed bath. Mary also likes to have her family/friends visit in the afternoon. On arrival Mary's visitors were offered afternoon tea and asked to wait in the visitors' room until Mary had her bed bath. This reduced the amount of time the visitors could spend with Mary. They were quite annoyed because they were kept waiting for so long and Mary was also very upset because she likes to shower in the morning, not in the afternoon. She was upset also because she had such a short time with her visitors; she looked forward to their visits so much. During the procedure (bed bath) Mary was not her usual chatty self and she was very grumpy. Mary expressed her dissatisfaction and annoyance by refusing to have her supper that evening.

Feelings: Uncomfortable feelings emerged for the carers concerned, knowing a shower in the morning rather than a bed bath would have been Mary's choice, having to hurry the procedure because Mary's visitors were waiting, not allowing enough time for the procedure, not informing Mary of the change in plan and not giving her the choice to have her shower in the morning. Uncomfortable feelings of guilt emerged for the carers involved because Mary and her visitors were deprived of spending quality time with her, also realising the distress the ordeal caused both physically and emotionally to Mary. This raised questions about the quality of client care and also the carers' feelings of dissatisfaction because they had let the client down.

Evaluation: Mary and her visitors suffered because of a management issue (staff shortage). The client's routine was disrupted and her individual rights were ignored because of organisational difficulties. The client's daily routine was reorganised, which cause her anxiety and upset her visitors; neither the client nor the visitors were given a choice. Mary's time with her visitors was cut short. However, Mary's hygiene was carried out which made her feel very comfortable and presentable for her visitors who were provided with afternoon tea in the visitor's room.

Analysis: The client and her visitors were very annoyed that they were disrupted and were not considered. They were expected to cooperate with the change of plan due to an organisational problem. The client and her visitors' rights were ignored and no apology was offered, which disregarded their rights as individuals. This caused unnecessary emotional distress, anxiety for Mary and annoyance for her visitors.

Conclusion: The issue regarding the change of plan should have been discussed with Mary beforehand. An explanation ought to have been provided; the reason why a bed bath was given in the afternoon should have been explained to Mary and maybe an agreement reached for a more suitable time for the task to be carried out, thereby ensuring that her visitors would not be kept waiting and extending Mary's quality time with them.

Action plan: Consider what action must be taken to improve future practice: prior planning of the morning routine, prioritising the workload, discussing the situation with the supervisor, requesting assistance to carry out the client's preferred hygiene routine of showering in the morning, thereby ensuring that the client was ready to receive afternoon visitors. Discuss with the client to involve them in the decision and agree a method and an appropriate time schedule to complete the task. Reassure the client that the inconvenience caused to her and her visitors will be avoided in future.

IMPLEMENTING KNOWLEDGE TO IMPROVE PERSONAL EFFECTIVENESS

- Implement knowledge gained through education and training. Introducing a system of reflective practice has been acknowledged as a method of improving personal effectiveness.
- *Benefits:* Reflecting on current/past experiences serves to identify gaps or lack of personal knowledge and forms the basis for directing and informing future practice. Reflection on practice is crucial in the stage of self-appraisal. It is a tool for evaluating the carer's personal performance in instances of client care. Using a structured model of reflection has been known to be very effective, e.g. reflective cycle (Gibbs, 1988).
- Knowledge gained through reflective education and training informs future practices. The carer must also consider how knowledge gained can be incorporated into and applied in practice.
- The application of improved knowledge and skills in the clinical setting is demonstrated through the process of giving deep consideration and thought to the task in hand, analysing and evaluating the content, drawing conclusions and taking action to provide the best possible outcome for the client.
- This structure also enables the carer to monitor and evaluate their own personal effectiveness by allowing them to identify their strengths and weaknesses.
- The knowledgeable carer provides a higher level of personal competence skills, which allows the carer to demonstrate skills with confidence in all aspects of client care.
- A more structured approach to care procedures improves communication between the client and the carer.

- Providing emotional, physical, social support and understanding for clients.
- Providing information to each client improves the carer's understanding of the client's feelings and allows the client to make an informed choice.
- Environmental reorganisation to facilitate client needs.
- Improved quality of client care: contented and satisfied clients and families; fewer complaints and also recognition of the establishment as an institution of quality in the provision of client care.

Assignment Guidelines

On completion of the FETAC Level 5 Care Support Module, candidates are required to submit the following:

A learner record: this must be compiled and submitted by candidates on completion of the module. The learner record should include a selection of evidence arising from candidates' work and interaction with others in a healthcare setting.

Assignment: candidates are required to produce and submit a practical activity from the workplace. This is prepared in consultation with a workplace supervisor. The activity should be planned, carried out and evaluated by the candidate. The activity may take the form of an outing or a social event for the client.

CHAPTER THREE

CARE SKILLS

Mary Power

Safe Environment; Communication; Breathing; Eating and Drinking; Elimination; Personal Hygiene and Dressing; Controlling Body Temperature; Mobilising; Work and Recreation; Expressing Sexuality; Sleep; Dying; Pressure-sore Prevention

Introduction

Identification of clients' needs following a holistic assessment must be carried out utilising the 'activities of living' (AL) framework. However, to implement and provide the care required, carers must have the knowledge and the appropriate skills to meet clients' assessed needs. In this chapter the care skills required will be discussed and described in great detail, using a systematic structured approach of care delivery (AL framework) based on the theoretical information described in chapter 2.

Lifespan is the period from conception until death. During any lifespan an individual develops along the dependence–independence continuum with different levels of dependence occurring at different periods of the lifespan. For example, a baby (infant) will be independent in the activity of breathing but will be dependent for food and nutrition until later on in life.

As a person progresses along the lifespan there may be movement towards dependence again. Factors such as age, chronic illness, disease or disability may reduce the independence of an individual in any of the twelve activities of living (ALs).

During a period of dependence the client may be unable to carry out their normal daily functions or 'activities of living'; therefore assistance will be required. It is generally accepted that the carer's personal beliefs, knowledge and attitudes regarding the individual's human needs are central to each client's individuality (Newton, 1991).

Implementing care for the dependent client within the twelve ALs ensures that a systematic approach of care delivery can be provided.

Safe Environment

Shelter

Shelter in the healthcare institution is provided when a proper environment is provided. This includes a bed that is comfortable and secure, where safety rails are in position if necessary, and where the client is kept warm and comfortable. This provides the client with a real sense of security and protection.

Safety needs

Clients must be provided with safety, protection, freedom from fear and anxiety, stability, order and security in their everyday lives. Clients become dependent on others to fulfil their safety needs if they lose their independence due to the following conditions:

- *Loss of memory*: can lead to forgetfulness, e.g. leaving burning cigarettes that may cause a fire, not turning off cookers, wandering around unfamiliar surroundings, not closing the front door. Clients with memory loss must be supervised and watched closely at all times to protect them from danger.
- *Failing eyesight*: poor vision causes increased falls, failure to see approaching traffic, failure to see warning signs and being unable to read or watch television. The carer must always ensure that clients with poor eyesight wear their prescribed glasses, which will provide protection in most situations, and remove obstacles within the environment to avoid accidents.
- *Diminished sense of smell*: unable to smell dangerous gasses or burning. Always ensure that the client is supervised and all appliances are checked regularly for faults.
- *Loss of hearing*: unable to hear the telephone, finds it difficult to become involved in conversation, unable to hear hazards, e.g. approaching traffic. Supervision is required to ensure the safety of the client. In situations of deafness the client should be referred to the medical doctor who may arrange for a hearing aid.
- *Failing sense of touch*: unable to feel hot appliances that may cause burning on the skin or unable to feel the cold and, in severe cases can develop hypothermia.
- *Clients with diminishing senses*: this occurs mostly in the older person, who must be supervised at all times for their own safety.
- *Confused and agitated clients*: must be protected at all times for their own safety. They may attempt to get out of bed or chair unaided and fall. Restraints are sometimes used but only with the permission of the client/family. However, restraints must always be therapeutic and never punitive. All healthcare facilities have policies in place to ensure the safety of this particular type of client, so it is imperative for the carer to follow local policy.
- *Infection control*: All healthcare facilities will have infection-control policies in order

to ensure that clients are not at risk of contracting infections (cross-infection). Carers have a personal responsibility to ensure that the infection-control policy is adhered to at all times to protect the client, i.e. handwashing as directed before moving from one client to another, following completion of all procedures. Ensure that all soiled garments and bed linen are disposed of according to protocol. Ensure that the environment is clean and dry (e.g. floors, baths, showers and toilets) after use. The carer must always wear protective clothing (gown/gloves) when caring for clients with infection or when handling or disposing of excreted body fluids. Furthermore, it is crucial that the local policy for infection control is adhered too at all times to prevent cross-infection.

Communication

Identify the client's usual form of communication and social interaction. The effects of illness or disability may cause the client to experience difficulty with any of the special senses: hearing, sight, speech, touch, smell. This will make communication very difficult. Therefore there may be a need for the carer to support the client's efforts to communicate in this regard. For example, clients recovering from a stroke may not be able to communicate in their usual form; they may be unable to speak as a result of the stroke. Always listen to what they are trying to say and never rush them; help them by trying to understand what they are saying.

CLIENT ANXIETY

Anxiety can exist in many people but may be expressed in many different forms, e.g. some clients may become very difficult and uncooperative due to fear of the unknown and the uncertainty of what may happen to them; others may become withdrawn and refuse to integrate with others. To alleviate the client's anxieties: try to get them to express their feelings; offer support; listen carefully to their response; give them time to answer; and do not rush them.

Clients surrender quite a lot of their privacy when they become dependent and place their health and wellbeing in the hands of the caregivers; they expect their personal rights to be protected. Intimate procedures should be provided for the client with discretion and in a manner that neither embarrasses nor exposes them unnecessarily. Always secure privacy, i.e. close the bed screens before performing any procedure and knock before entering the client's room. Ensure privacy is provided when attending to the client's personal needs. The client must also feel that they can trust the carer with personal information. Add to the client's sense of security by treating them with courtesy, always remembering to treat each client as a unique individual.

Emotional needs

Emotional needs are the same at all levels of the lifespan of each person. Everyone needs to be loved and to love others in return. The normal expectation is to be treated with respect and dignity and to feel that self-esteem is protected. Many people have a vision of how they wish to appear to others; this idea is referred to as self-esteem. For example, some clients may project themselves to those around them as self-reliant and independent, capable of making all decisions regarding themselves and their family. However, this can change very suddenly with the onset of an acute illness, which can render an individual very dependent and reliant on others to perform the most basic of physical functions. These circumstances threaten even the most secure person's self-esteem. How clients respond when their self-esteem is threatened depends on the individual and their ability to cope with the feeling of helplessness, but also it depends on the carer's ability to understand and identify with the client's situation. Some clients may feel frustrated and angry and complain a lot, while others may become withdrawn and quiet but will be cooperative and non-complaining. This may be a false front to hide the fear of not being able to cope with the situation they find themselves in. Carers must try to identify these feelings and provide the necessary support for the client.

Spiritual needs

Some clients may be more spiritual than others; some may hold strong religious beliefs, whereas others may not have any at all. Personal beliefs must never be forced on clients. Each person has a right to a religious preference or to deny the existence of any beliefs. The client may express a wish to visit a chaplain or a clergy service, so the carer should always ensure to make this service available to them. Some clients may also wish to attend a religious service. Most facilities have religious services available at particular times. Try to assist the client to attend and provide support if necessary.

Breathing

Oxygen/Air

All of us need oxygen to survive; we cannot live without it. The carer will encounter many clients with breathing difficulties, perhaps due to medical conditions. Therefore they may be unable to inhale (breathe in) sufficient oxygen to maintain the body's needs during inspiration, or may be unable to exhale carbon dioxide during expiration. Oxygen makes up 21 per cent of fresh air, but many clients who suffer from respiratory or cardiac diseases will need much higher percentages of oxygen to survive. Respiratory-compromised clients require increased amounts of oxygen; this can be provided through nasal prongs or an oxygen facemask attached to an oxygen supply system. This must only be carried out on the instructions of, or delegated by, the registered nurse.

The client with breathing difficulty must be sitting up in bed and supported with a backrest and pillows. This will make respiration (breathing) easier. Where possible, the client should be encouraged to do regular breathing exercises to keep the airways clear and allow oxygen to flow freely to the lungs. The carer must observe the client's colour, body temperature and the rate of breathing per minute continuously.

Eating and Drinking

FOOD/NUTRITION

Dependent clients may be reluctant or unable to eat an adequate amount of food to maintain a stable diet. Lack of appetite may be due to the fact that they are in a healthcare facility or perhaps they are uncomfortable, anxious or they don't like the food available. However, it may also be due to a medical condition or just age. Whatever the reason, lack of appetite must always be reported to the supervisor. Some clients may need alternative methods of feeding because of their disability. Others may need special food products (diets), e.g. diabetics. Liquidised food must be provided for clients with difficulty in chewing.

Alternative feeding routes include the following:

- Clients who are unable to eat food in the usual way must be fed through alternative routes, i.e. intravenously or via a fine-bore nasal tube (naso-gastric tube). This tube is passed through the nasal passages and the oesophagus and sited in the stomach, or through a tube that is placed directly into the stomach or small bowel through the abdominal wall. Food given in this way is specially prepared and always administered by an experienced professional; however, the carer may be asked to assist with this procedure from time to time.

- Intravenous infusion is used to replace fluids and avoid dehydration. This is administered through a cannula inserted into one of the large veins, usually in the upper limbs. The intravenous method is also used to administer 'Total Parenteral Nutrition' (TPN), total nutrition if infused through a major vessel (vein) following the insertion of a fine catheter. These are specialist procedures and the administrators of food through alternative routes must have the knowledge and expertise and be deemed competent to carry out these tasks.

Nutrition can be administered to clients in many different ways, but the requirements of each client must be addressed individually. Whatever method of administration is required, there are general points that must be observed and these include the following principles:

- Ensure that the food is served in comfortable, clean surroundings.
- Offensive odours must be curtailed as much as possible, e.g. close bathroom/toilet doors.
- Equipment not in use should be removed, e.g. commode.
- The client should be prepared, i.e. sitting up, and the bed table correctly positioned.
- Allow the client to wash his/her hands.
- Presentation of the tray and arrangement of food must look appetising to stimulate the appetite.
- Ensure the food is at the correct temperature.
- Clients should be encouraged to help themselves as much as possible, but offer assistance when necessary.

Elimination

Regular excretion of waste products is essential to maintain a healthy, active body. Waste products contain a certain amount of toxins that will damage the client's health if they are not excreted. The healthy body has the ability to rid itself of waste products through perspiration (sweating), excretion of urine from the kidneys, faeces from the rectum, and carbon dioxide from the lungs when the person breathes out (exhales).

Promoting Elimination

Encourage the client to drink plenty of fluids and offer a high-fibre diet to avoid constipation.

Bathing and maintaining personal hygiene will encourage perspiration. Wash and dry the skin well to keep the pores clean and healthy.

Assisted Urinary Drainage

Additional assistance may be required for some clients who suffer from conditions of the urinary tract and are unable to pass urine normally. A sterile catheter is inserted into the bladder to provide continuous drainage of urine. The catheter can be attached to a sealed collection bag and the urine is drained at least twice daily, or more often if necessary. Always wear protective gloves when draining a urine bag. Note the colour, consistency and odour of the urine and measure the amount. Release the clip and allow the contents to flow into a measuring container for this purpose, and dispose of same according to local policy. Ensure that the measuring container is sterilised, remove gloves and wash hands, report findings and document if appropriate.

Assisted faecal evacuation

Oral medication can be an effective and gentle option in the administration of a laxative to assist in the evacuation of faeces from the bowel. Otherwise, a mild laxative can be administrated directly into the rectum to encourage faecal evacuation. However, all of these remedies must be prescribed by the doctor and administered by qualified personnel with the consent of the client.

Other methods of assisting faecal evacuation include management of a stoma, i.e. colostomy or illeostomy. A stoma is an opening into the bowel. This opening is attached to the abdominal wall and secured onto the skin surface. The opening allows the contents of the bowel (faeces) to be excreted. A special collection bag is attached to the stoma on the abdomen. This condition is associated with clients who have medical diseases of the colon (bowel).

Assist clients who are unable to use the toilet facilities by providing them with commodes, bedpans or urinals.

Assisting clients with elimination is a very personal procedure. Therefore every effort must be made to protect client privacy and avoid embarrassment.

- Ensure privacy is secured, i.e. close screens/doors. If the client's condition allows, leave the room open until the client has completed, leaving a call bell close at hand.
- Wear protective clothing and provide bedpan/urinal promptly at the client's request. Help the client to position bedpan/urinal. Allow the client sufficient time, and remain within close proximity.
- When the client has finished remove bedpan/ urinal. Observe contents and dispose of same as instructed. Ensure all utensils are placed in the steriliser and disposed of according to local policy.
- Wash and dry the client's hands and genital area and discreetly remove protective clothing and gloves. Wash hands before opening the screens.

INCONTINENCE

Incontinence is the inability to control the passing of urine and bowel movements. It may be caused by physical or emotional problems or due to medication. Incontinence is considered to be a serious condition as it can cause social isolation and indignity for the person with the problem. There are two types of incontinence: urinary incontinence and faecal incontinence. Urinary incontinence is more common than faecal incontinence.

Urinary Incontinence: can affect all ages, there is an urgency to pass urine from the bladder more frequently than normal. This is a condition where urine is passed involuntarily to such a degree that it is socially and hygienically unacceptable for the client. There are many different types of urinary incontinence: it can be due, for example, to pelvic-floor muscle weakness or urinary tract infection. Correct diagnosis is important as, more often than not, it is the symptom of an underlying medical condition. Problems occur when the increased need to empty the bladder is combined with loss of mobility or physical impairment, and the toilet is not within close proximity to the client.

Faecal (bowel) incontinence: faecal incontinence is a problem that can affect any age group but is most prevalent in the older person. It is mainly caused by an abnormality and weakness of the external anal sphincter and the pelvic-floor muscles, which causes the bowel motion to flow out without control through the muscle of the back passage (rectum). Incontinence of faeces can also be caused by medical conditions of the bowel, nerve damage during childbirth, certain medications and unconsciousness.

MANAGING INCONTINENCE

- Clients with incontinence can be helped by toileting at regular intervals.
- Ensure privacy is secured for the client; close door and bed screens.
- Always help the client to the toilet promptly when called.
- A raised toilet seat can be very useful; a commode can be very convenient for clients who are confined to bed.
- Faecal incontinence may be helped with diet regulation. This has been very successful in some cases.
- Protective appliances may be used to avoid embarrassment for the client.
- Protect the surrounding skin areas with creams to prevent rashes or ulceration of the skin.
- Advice from a continence advisor is always very worthwhile; generally they provide excellent advice on appropriate individual management and should always be involved in these situations.

Personal Hygiene and Dressing

Establish the client's usual pattern of hygiene and dressing if possible. Also, identify whether or not the client needs assistance, and establish if there is some level of dependence. Provide the client with choice of a bath, shower or bed bath. Observe the condition of the skin, e.g. any areas of redness; this may be an indication of the development of pressure sores. Check for any skin rash, swelling, scars or abrasions. Discreetly check for any body lice or head lice. Always respect the client's wishes with regard to the type of clothing they wish to wear and only make suggestions if asked.

ASSISTING CLIENTS WITH HYGIENE NEEDS

- Explain the procedure to the client and get the client's agreement. Thorough hand washing is necessary to prevent cross-infection.
- Collect the toiletries for the bath/shower.
- Ensure the equipment and environment are clean.

- Remove all sensory aids – glasses, hearing aids, dentures – before commencing procedure.
- Offer toilet facility to the client.
- Close all windows and doors and ensure the environment is warm.
- Ensure the protection of any attachments, i.e. catheters, oxygen/urinary/feeding tubes.
- Help the client to remove clothing.
- Check the temperature of the water.
- Allow the client to wash any part of their body if they wish.
- Communicate normally with the client during the procedure.
- Start at the head and face and work downwards towards the feet.
- Expose only the necessary parts of the body; cover with a towel as soon as possible.
- Always wash genital area last; the client may wish to wash this area. Use a separate sponge for this purpose and disposable gloves.
- Call assistance to move the client from the bath/shower if necessary.
- Ensure the client's body is thoroughly dried.
- Apply moisturising cream or talcum powder according to the client's wishes.
- Assist with dressing the client with freshly laundered clothes. Ensure the client is satisfied with the suggested choice of clothing, ensure all zips and buttons are fastened and shoes are laced and tied properly.
- Dry and brush the hair to the client's satisfaction.
- Position the client in a comfortable position in bed/chair.
- Dispose of all soiled linen/towels according to institution policy.
- Clean all equipment used in the procedure and store away safely.
- Wash hands thoroughly.

COMPLETE BED BATH

A complete bed bath involves washing the client's entire body. Always explain the procedure and get the client's permission. It is essential for some clients who are unable to shower or bathe in the normal way to be given a bed bath to maintain personal hygiene. Collect all the necessary articles to carry out the bed bath and arrange on a trolley close to the bedside.

- Secure privacy; shut all windows and doors.
- Lay the client flat, lying on back with one pillow if tolerated.
- Cover the client's body with a bath blanket. Remove the bed linen and the client's nightwear and place in the container for laundering.
- Ensure the washbasin is two-thirds full of tepid water and place the towel over the client's chest.

- Gently wash the face, the eyes, the neck and the ears with face towel and gently dry.
- Place the bath towel under the far armpit. Support the arm and wash the shoulder, armpit, upper and lower arm, and dry.
- Place the washbasin on the towel and place the client's hand into the basin and wash and dry well. Repeat the procedure for the near arm.
- Place the bath towel over the chest crossways and pull down the bath blanket from under the towel to the waist. Lift the towel slightly and wash the chest, taking care not to expose the body unnecessarily. Rinse and dry well, especially under the breasts and folds of skin.
- Move the towel lengthways to cover the chest and abdomen. Pull the bath blanket down over the pubic area, and lift the towel slightly and wash and dry the abdomen.
- Pull the bath blanket back up to the shoulders, covering the front of the body and both arms. Remove the towel and change the water if necessary.
- Place the bath towel lengthways under the far leg and foot, keeping the genital area covered. Bend the knee and wash and dry the leg. Wash and dry the foot, paying particular attention between the toes. Remove the towel and cover the near leg and repeat the procedure.
- Turn the client on his/her side, keeping the body covered with the bath blanket.
- Uncover the back and buttocks and place the bath towel on the bed. Wash the back, working from the neck down to the end of the buttocks and dry well. Place the client on his/her back.
- Gently separate the legs to wash the genital area. Place a towel underneath the buttocks. The client may wish to wash this area. Use a separate cloth for this area and make sure the area is dried well. Always allow the client to do as much as possible to encourage independence.
- Change the bed linen and the client's nightwear and place the client in a comfortable position.
- Dispose of all articles to be discarded as per local policy.
- Ensure all articles used in the procedure are washed, cleaned and stored away.

ORAL HYGIENE

Cleaning the client's teeth

- Explain the procedure to the client and wash hands.
- Collect the required utensils; toothbrush/paste, mouthwash, glass of water, bowl, face towel, disposable gloves, paper towels.
- Position the client in the sitting position. Place the towel over the chest.
- Put the disposable gloves on and apply the toothpaste to the toothbrush. Hold over the bowl and pour a small amount of water over the brush.

- Ask the client to open their mouth widely. Insert the brush into the mouth and brush the upper and lower teeth gently. Offer a rinse with water and hold a bowl under the client's chin to spit into; repeat rinse if necessary. Dry the client's mouth with paper towels. Remove the bowl and discard the contents. Remove gloves and discard, then wash hands.

Cleaning the client's dentures

Dentures must be cleaned as often as natural teeth. However, unlike natural teeth, dentures are slippery when wet; they can fall easily and chip if dropped on hard surfaces. Therefore it is essential to hold dentures firmly with the gloved hand over a bowl of cold water when brushing. When clean, place back into the client's mouth or place in a container of cold water specifically for this purpose. Always use the gloved hand to remove or reinsert the dentures if the client is unable to do this task.

Controlling Body Temperature

Observe the temperature of the body. Never uncover the client's body unnecessarily. Make sure the client has sufficient clothing to keep the body at a comfortable temperature. If the client feels very hot, remove some of the clothing or bed covering and report this to the registered nurse; the client may be developing an underlying infection. The central heating may need to be adjusted to suit the client if necessary.

Mobilising

Physical activity is a natural part of a normal human lifestyle, but illness or disability limits activity. For example, if the client is confined to bed for a period of time because of an illness, their physical activity is limited. Prolonged inactivity can cause complications of a very serious nature that can be very damaging with long-term effects. Therefore it is essential to establish the capability of the client in this regard.

Promoting physical activity generally improves the functioning of all systems, and muscle tone and joints function more effectively. Circulation and respiration are increased and the whole body reacts in a very positive way to physical activity. However, many clients may still need some degree of assistance with physical activity. Always ensure that walking aids and assistance are available. This enables clients to maintain their independence for as long as possible. The carer role is very important and can be very effective by supporting and encouraging clients to mobilise on a regular basis, e.g. take a short walk in the morning and the afternoon with assistance. Assisting the client to mobilise relieves their anxiety and fear of falling. Always walk on either side of or behind the client; for unsteady clients give them a walking aid and stand directly behind them. If the client is using a walking stick, exercise the client by holding one arm securely, placing your other arm around the client's waist if they are nervous or anxious. A regular daily exercise routine is generally found to be a very worthwhile. It not only keeps the client physically active, but also has a positive effect on their social wellbeing by helping to keep them involved.

COMPLICATIONS OF INACTIVITY

- *Loss of muscle strength and tone*: perform a range of motion activities as ordered.
- *Formation of blood clots*: check for discolouration of the skin of lower limbs (e.g. redness, temperature, swelling or pain). Report all findings.
- *Development of contractures*: perform motion exercises gently; position the body in proper alignment with appropriate support, change position frequently as instructed.
- *Fluid or electrolyte imbalance*: observe client's intake and urinary output. Encourage the intake of fluids and report signs of fluid retention.
- *Reduced cardiac and respiratory function*: observe colour, respiration and any signs of sweating. Change position as instructed, encouraging deep breathing and coughing. Sit the client up, supported with pillows. Report findings.
- *Infection*: observe for signs of infection such as sweating, rapid heart rate, rapid breathing rate or cough.
- *Loss of appetite*: encourage food intake. Assist with feeding if necessary and order special diet as requested by the client.
- *Constipation*: report bowel motions. Give laxative as instructed, provide assistance and privacy.
- *Skin breakdown*: wash and dry skin. Frequently apply protective lotion, keep skin soft and prevent cracks developing. Change position as required and use pressure-relieving equipment. Report evidence of skin breakdown, e.g. emergence of pressure sores.
- *Altered behaviour*: always try to understand how the client is feeling. Listen to what they are saying and try to calm them. Assist in any way possible to alleviate any frustrations expressed by the client.

Work and Recreation

SOCIAL NEEDS

Social needs and activities are unique to each person; these activities provide the feel-good factor, improve self-esteem and promote a sense of achievement.

Sociological needs are achieved by interacting with other people, which provides the opportunity for free personal expression. One of the most basic needs for humans is the need to be understood and to understand others; this is achieved through successful communication with others.

Communication usually occurs verbally, but this can also be conveyed through body language, facial expressions and tone of voice. Social interaction with visitors or other clients may satisfy the client's need to communicate effectively. This must always be encouraged.

- Identify the client's special interests, past and present, and support the client in every way possible in the pursuit of those interests. Discuss social needs with the individual client and make it easier from them to express their wishes. This also makes it easier for carers to find correct ways to fulfil clients' social needs.
- Encourage the client to become involved in the social activities available. Providing enjoyable pastimes for the client, alone or with others, breaks the daily routine, rebuilds self-esteem and helps form new relationships.
- With the help of others, organise social outings, e.g. musical evenings, bingo sessions or card-playing events.
- Inform the client about upcoming events and encourage them to become involved. Make the necessary arrangements and ensure that the client can be transported with assistance if necessary.
- Allow the client to decide whether or not they want to participate and always respect their wishes.

Expressing Sexuality

INTIMACY

Intimacy is a feeling of closeness to another person with whom one has a relationship marked by feelings of love. Friends, lovers and family can share intimacy; there is also a degree of intimacy established between the client and the carer when they learn to trust one another. Intimate relationships may be expressed in different ways, depending on preference, opportunity and moral standards.

Sexual behaviour is a personal choice and intimacy is an important aspect of the human sexual experience. It is important to understand that not all humans have the same sexual preferences. This does not mean that difference makes one person wrong and another person right. Carers are expected to understand clients who may not share their personal views.

HUMAN TOUCH

The need for human touch must never be underestimated. Age groups from infancy to old age experience the same human feelings. Human touch generates feelings of comfort, security and satisfaction for all. The need for human touch does not change with age, i.e. during the adult years the need for human touch is reserved for close friends and family, but life circumstances change and the opportunity for touching decreases. This can make the client feel isolated, deprived and forgotten about and can cause extreme loneliness and depression. This is especially true when a person lives alone or is in a long-term care facility. A friendly smile, a pat on the shoulder or gently holding a person's hand can satisfy a lonely person's need for human contact. Care must be taken not to give the wrong impression or to overdo or force personal attentions upon a client, but the friendly human touch can mean so much to the wellbeing of clients.

Sleep

Sufficient sleep each night is essential for all clients. Sleep deprivation can have serious consequences for some clients in a healthcare facility. Therefore every effort must be made to ensure that clients get an adequate night's sleep. Noise, pain and emotional stress are the most common reasons why clients have difficulty sleeping.

The following general rules may help to induce sleep for clients:

- Reduce noise whenever possible.
- Avoid handling equipment.
- Reduce the volume of radio and television.
- Limit unnecessary conversation with others and modify the voice volume when speaking.
- Close the client's door and all doors leading to the exits of the institution.
- Ensure that the client is in a comfortable position and prepared for a restful night's sleep before the registered nurse administers the night sedative. This avoids the client being further disturbed.
- However, if the client has concerns or is worried about their medical condition and the outcome, the carer will not have the answers to their questions. Listen to what they are saying, show compassion and give reassurance while endeavouring to understand their situation. Offer support and get a professional member of staff to discuss the issues with them as soon as possible. While it will not be possible to eliminate the client's concerns, it may be possible to alleviate their anxiety in the short term. A reduction in anxiety will help the client to rest easier.

Dying

Each individual will have his or her own beliefs about the hereafter. Some may be worried and have fears. Provide support and ask the client if they wish to speak to the pastoral care team or the palliative care team who are the specialists in the care of the dying. Sometimes a client may wish for a relative or a member of staff to sit and listen or talk with them during the process of dying. Always make sure the family is kept informed about any expressed wish of the client or message they may want passed on. This topic is covered in greater detail in Chapter 9 (Palliative Care Support).

Pressure-sore Prevention

A pressure sore is an area of localised damage to the skin and underlying tissue triggered by pressure, shear or friction or a combination of all these. This causes lack of oxygen and blood to the tissues resulting in possible destruction and ulceration. Therefore a pressure sore develops as a direct result of damage to localised areas of the skin caused by pressure occurring between the bony prominence on the inside and a resistant surface on the outside, i.e. mattress or chair. Pressure sores not only jeopardise the health status of clients, they also carry underlying connotations of neglect, mismanagement and feelings of guilt on the part of the care providers (Beckmann, 1995). Consequently it is essential that a policy for the prevention of pressure sores exists in all institutions providing client care.

The skin is the largest organ of the human body. Covering the entire body surface, it is made up of the epidermis (the surface layer, which protects the body from bacteria) and the dermis layer, which contains fibrous tissue, blood vessels and nerves. The deeper layer of the dermis contains sweat glands and hair follicles.

FUNCTIONS OF THE SKIN

The skin has many functions: it covers and protects the surface of the body; prevents the entry of infection; assists in regulation of the body temperature; eliminates small amounts of waste products and has slight absorption facilities; it is also highly sensitive to touch.

The sick and disabled are particularly susceptible to the development of pressure sores. This is mainly due to their physiological condition because of their inability to mobilise as they maybe confined to bed. The application of pressure to the skin's surface for a prolonged period of time occludes the underlying blood supply to the tissues. This has the potential to cause serious damage to the skin of a client who is confined to bed or immobile for a period of time. Therefore the pressure must be relieved to allow reperfusion (restoration of blood flow) to the affected area and avoid destruction of the underlying tissue.

CAUSES OF TISSUE BREAKDOWN

It is necessary to understand the causes of tissue breakdown in order to implement a plan for prevention of pressure sores.

Pressure sores can be caused by a number of factors; venerable people who are immobile, those who have reduced sensation and have certain medical conditions are susceptible. There must also be physical force which affects the tissue; pressure and other factors, including social circumstance, availability of resources and the environment in which the client is cared for. The predisposing factors to pressure-sore formation can be further classified into intrinsic and extrinsic factors (Braden & Bergstrom, 1987).

Extrinsic Factors: are those external influences in the client's physical environment that contribute to the development of a pressure sore (Pang & Wong, 1998).

- Shear-tissue destruction occurs when the skin is dragged in opposite directions. This causes distortion and stretching and tearing of the blood capillaries, i.e. this occurs when the client slides down from the sitting position.
- Friction-tissue destruction from resistance to movement of skin against another surface results in an abrasion of the skin and can occur when incorrect manual handling technique is used, e.g. dragging the client up the bed.
- Maceration: tissue destruction when the skin is exposed to moisture, i.e. body fluids, urine and faeces, makes the skin softer when exposed to moisture and more vulnerable to other destructive forces (Torrance, 1988).
- The main extrinsic factor in the development of pressure sores is pressure because it gives rise to distortion and occlusion of blood vessels supplying the tissues overlying a bony prominence. There is no absolute pressure at which damage may occur, nor is there a definite period of time; it can vary from person to person as other factors come into play.

Intrinsic factors: are characteristics of the person that increase his/her susceptibility to pressure-sore development, for example poor nutrition, blood pressure, incontinence, sensory perception, level of mobility, age, gender, body mass, and medical conditions such as poor circulation, diabetes, generalised infections, drug therapy, psychological and social factors.

IDENTIFICATION OF PRESSURE POINTS

Any part of the body where the skin's soft tissue is compressed between a bony prominence and an external surface is at risk. Specific points of the body have been identified as high risk when the client is lying in certain positions. These include:

- *Lying position*: toes, heels, buttocks, sacrum, spinal column (backbone) shoulder blades, back of the head and the elbows all are at risk of developing pressure sores in this position.
- *Lateral position*: heels, ankles, outer and inner aspects of the knees, hips, elbows, tip of shoulder, ears and the side of the head are all at risk.
- *Sitting up position*: the buttocks and sacrum are most at risk.

CLASSIFICATION OF PRESSURE SORES

Any lesion caused by unrelieved pressure resulting in damage to the skin and surrounding tissues is defined as a pressure sore, classified into four grades depending on severity:

Grade 1: the skin feels warm to the touch, looks discoloured and is swollen and hard.

Grade 2: partial skin loss involving the outer and under layer of the skin. The pressure sore is superficial and presents clinically as an abrasion or blister on the skin.

Grade 3: full thickness skin loss which may extend down to the muscle.

Grade4: involves extensive tissue destruction, damage to muscle and bone and supporting structures.

Procedure for prevention of pressure sores

It is widely believed that care is the primary measure in the prevention of pressure-sore formation (David, Chapman & Lockett, 1983). There are three main elements involved in the prevention of pressure sores. The primary source of information of a developing pressure sore is gained from a comprehensive assessment of the client. The importance of early detection and identification of clients at risk of developing pressure sores cannot be overemphasised. Therefore initial assessment and reassessment of clients at risk must be conducted regularly and all predisposing factors affecting the client must be factored into the equation. There are various assessment tools, e.g. Waterlow, Braden and Norton, used by practicing healthcare professionals to assess people at risk. These tools facilitate the prediction of the emergence and grading of pressure sores.

Repositioning: turning the client to relieve pressure is essential and must be carried out on a regular basis. Repositioning of clients is based on the assessment, the individual's tolerance to immobility and individual need. When repositioning a client, always ensure correct manual handling techniques are used (refer to Chapter 4) while at the same time protecting the client from shear and friction.

Pressure-relieving surfaces: the primary benefit is in the management of the extrinsic factors, i.e. pressure shear friction (Barnett & Shelton, 1997). Pressure-relieving surfaces are available in the form of pressure-relieving mattresses and cushions. These appliances are essential in the prevention and treatment of pressure sores and must be available to clients at risk. They are designed to relieve, reduce and distribute pressure; however, they must be used in conjunction with a repositioning schedule plan of care based on individual client need. Bed covers, e.g. duvets and blankets, must be supported and loosely covering the body and lower limbs.

Clients sitting out of bed in a chair are also at risk and must be provided with a pressure-relieving cushion. Relief of pressure when sitting is essential. It is also vital to stand the client or take short walks if the client's condition permits. Periods spent immobile, sitting in a chair, should be limited to two hours at any one time. Always ensure that the client adopts the optimal sitting position, which includes correct chair height; correct depth and width of seat; back, foot and thigh support; feet uncrossed and correct body posture.

Regular assessment of the client's nutritional status is important: weight measurements, skin assessments and recording of food and fluid intake. If the client has insufficient nutritional intake, their skin will break down much quicker and take longer to recover. Body hygiene, which includes skincare, must be attended to on a regular basis and the promotion of continence will help to maintain the integrity of the skin. It is necessary always to be observant when carrying out personal hygiene or dressing clients. Report any unusual redness, swelling or discolouration of the skin to the supervisor.

The presence of a pressure sore has very serious consequences for the client concerned, the healthcare team and the institution. A pressure sore causes great pain, discomfort and suffering for the client. It can isolate the client from society and recovery can be long and slow. Indeed some clients may never fully recover from the traumatic experience. Furthermore the development of a pressure sore is very often viewed as a reflection of the quality of the care provided. However, this is not always the case as so many factors come into play, e.g. the monetary cost of treatment, and staff time can be extremely expensive for the healthcare institution. Finally the problem of pressure sores has been a challenge to healthcare professionals for centuries. Following an extensive amount of research carried out on this subject, it is believed that care is the primary measure to prevent pressure-sore formation. If those at risk can be predicted, care can be directed towards them, thereby preventing unnecessary complications and suffering as well as saving considerable costs (Flanagan, 1993). Consequently it is essential that every effort is made to prevent the development of pressure sores which will benefit all concerned and improve society's confidence in the care provided.

Assignment guidelines

Candidates are assessed demonstrating three practical skills. Candidates are also expected to submit two assignments: each assignment should focus on an aspect of client care with reference to the needs of the client, the level of assistance required and the course of action taken.

CHAPTER FOUR

SAFETY AND HEALTH AT WORK

Vanessa Griffin-Heslin

Legislation Relating to Safety and Health in the Republic of Ireland; Safety Statements; Risk Assessment, Hazards and Risks; The Health and Safety Authority; Safe and Healthy Work Environments; Fire; Infection Control; First Aid; Manual Handling; Risk Factors in Relation to Health; Conclusion

Introduction

This chapter discusses factors relating to safety and health in healthcare settings. The advice and information can be applied to various settings, including hospitals, community settings and nursing homes. The chapter aims to assist students who are studying for the FETAC Level 5 Certificate in Healthcare Support where Safety and Health at Work is one of the modules. Legislation requires both employers and employees to perform certain duties to ensure the safety and health of patients, visitors and staff. Safety and health is everybody's responsibility and no one can afford to turn a blind eye to it. Effective communication and excellent training in safety and health help to ensure a safe and effective working environment, without which accidents causing injury or even death will happen.

Legislation Relating to Safety and Health in the Republic of Ireland

Safety and health at work in the Republic of Ireland is governed by legislation. Prior to the 1989 Safety, Health and Welfare at Work Act, there appeared little in the way of legislation governing safety in the workplace.

The main aim of the 1989 Act was to focus on ways to prevent accidents and ill health. It applied to employers, employees and self-employed people. The basis of the Act was risk assessment, safety statements, employers' and employees' duties. This Act was amended in 2005 and is the current legislation for safety and health in the workplace in the Republic of Ireland.

GENERAL DUTIES OF THE EMPLOYER

Sections 8–11 of the Safety, Health and Welfare at Work Act 2005 list the general duties required of employers. Some of these are:

- To ensure the safety, health and welfare of their employees by providing and maintaining a workplace that is as safe as possible with minimal risk to health.
- To prevent improper conduct and behaviour in the workplace.
- To provide health and safety information and training to employees, using language that can be understood by all.
- To eliminate hazards or reduce them to the absolute minimum by carrying out assessment of risks in all areas of work.
- To issue and keep updated safety statements that include health and safety policy and procedures for the workplace.
- To provide protective clothing and equipment where appropriate, e.g. gloves, aprons, hoists for lifting patients.
- To provide welfare facilities, e.g. first-aid stations and trained first aiders.
- To put in place emergency plans, e.g. procedures to follow in case of fire.

GENERAL DUTIES OF THE EMPLOYEE

Section 13 identifies the general duties of an employee. These include the following:

- To ensure they take reasonable care to protect their safety and that of any other person who may be affected by acts of omission.
- To avoid being under the influence of an intoxicant, as this can seriously impair a person's judgment and can lead to dangerous, even fatal, consequences.
- To cooperate with employer to assist in complying with health and safety legislation.
- To attend training, paying due regard to it and other instructions in their workplace.
- To report any unsafe working conditions to the employer or to the designated responsible person.

Safety Statements

Section 20 of the Safety, Health and Welfare at Work Act 2005 requires all employers and self-employed people to prepare a safety statement within the workplace. This is based on the principle that workplace-induced ill health and accidents are mostly avoidable and may be prevented if correct policies and procedures are in place and followed. A written safety statement should include hazard identification and risk assessment, the protective and preventative measures taken to ensure safety, health and welfare at work, the duties of his/her employees and the names, job titles and duties of each person responsible for performing tasks assigned to him or her. The safety statement is designed to benefit employees by safeguarding their health and safety in the workplace.

Risk Assessment, Hazards and Risks

Section 19 of the Safety, Health and Welfare at Work Act 2005 requires the employer to identify hazards and carry out a risk assessment in their workplace. The risk assessment involves examining what, in the workplace, could cause harm to people and whether or not there are enough precautions in place to prevent it. This includes the identification of hazards (anything that can cause harm) and risks (the likelihood of someone being harmed by the hazard and how severe the harm might be). Following on from this, the employer has the responsibility to take steps to implement any improvements considered necessary to guarantee the health and safety of all employees.

According to the Health and Safety Authority (2005) there are five steps to the risk assessment:

1. IDENTIFY THE HAZARDS

   A hazard is anything that can potentially cause harm. In a healthcare setting some of these may include:
   - Slips, trips and falls
   - Poor housekeeping
   - Fire
   - Manual handling
   - Infection control
   - Waste disposal (for example, clinical waste and needle sticks)
   - Human factors (examples of these include bullying, violence against staff, stress and long working hours)
   - Faulty electrical wiring and electrical equipment
   - Unsuitable levels of lighting

2. ASSESS THE RISKS

   A risk is the likelihood of the harm occurring and the severity of the consequences if it does. The employer must assess if a risk is high, medium or low; for example, an injury from manual handling may create a high risk because it is carried out frequently and, if carried out incorrectly, can lead to serious injury.

3. SELECT THE CONTROL MEASURES

   The appropriate control measures to eliminate the hazards as far as possible must be reviewed. Completely eliminating all hazards may not, of course, always be entirely possible. Therefore the control measures put into place must reduce the risk of injury or effects to health to the absolute minimum. Examples of control measures would be the provision of a hoist to be used for manual handling, gloves to be worn to prevent the spread of infection and sharps bins to reduce the risk of needle-stick injuries.

4 . WRITE THE SAFETY STATEMENT

The employer, having carried out steps 1–3 above, must now write the safety statement. This would include the following details:
- Control measures to be taken to avoid the risks
- Name(s) of those responsible for implementing and maintaining the measures
- Places (and telephone numbers where appropriate) for dealing with an emergency
- The names of the safety representatives (if any) (The Health and Safety Authority, 2005)

5 . RECORD AND REVIEW

The safety statement must be kept under review. It must be updated should working conditions change or as and when new risks are identified. The Health and Safety Authority (2005) recommended that the safety statement be reviewed at least once a year.

The Health and Safety Authority (HSA)

The Health and Safety Authority (HSA) has responsibility for ensuring health and safety in the workplace in the Republic of Ireland. Among their many responsibilities, the HSA requires employers, employees and the general public to comply with health and safety regulations under the current Safety, Health and Welfare at Work Act 2005. They investigate any workplace accidents or causes of ill health and, where considered necessary, develop new laws and standards on health and safety at work. The HSA also provides information, carries out research, develops codes of practice and offers education and training in the field of safety and health at work (www.hsa.ie).

Safe and Healthy Work Environments

There are many safety issues within healthcare settings. Hazard identification is of the utmost importance to ensure the working environment remains as safe as possible and should be included within the risk assessment. However, it remains the personal responsibility of all staff to be vigilant for hazardous objects, materials and substances and to act accordingly to prevent injury. Excellent and effective communication – oral, written and training – plays a vital role in promoting a safe and healthy working environment. Under current legislation employers must ensure that staff members are offered the opportunity to attend training programmes, e.g. fire training and manual handling. For everyone's safety, employers should insist that employees attend the mandatory training. Employees must accept that they have a responsibility to attend the courses, take them seriously and put into practice what they learn.

Employees are also expected to act responsibly so as not to endanger themselves or others whilst they are in the workplace. The Safety, Health and Welfare at Work Act 2005 Section 13 states clearly that employees must ensure that they are not under the influence of an intoxicant (alcohol or drugs) to the extent that he or she will endanger their own safety and health or that of any other person. The effects of alcohol and drugs can seriously affect one's judgment, which could lead to potentially fatal consequences when dealing with patients.

Manual handling activities make up a large proportion of HCAs' work and this is often the cause of many employees' injuries, particularly those affecting the back. The Health and Safety Authority (2005) reported in 2003 that 34 per cent of reportable accidents had resulted in injuries as a result of a manual handling activity. This report does not specify what injuries were recorded, only that they were caused by manual handling activities. Employees, under the Safety, Health and Welfare at Work Act 2005 Section 13, are required to attend training sessions to protect their own safety, health and welfare and this would, of course, include manual handling courses.

Wet floors, poor maintenance, faulty electrical equipment and wiring, objects left lying around and poor housekeeping are all hazards that can cause injury to staff, visitors and patients. They are all hazards that can be identified in the working environment by alert and vigilant staff members who have been trained to recognise them.

According to Benson (2000), excellent security, such as locks on doors, intercom systems, closing lower ground windows, good lighting in car parks and in corridors and a security guard (if possible), can help to keep staff, visitors and patients as secure as possible. All staff must wear name badges so they can be identifiable at all times to minimise the risk of unauthorised intruders.

Effective housekeeping can eliminate some workplace hazards and prevent accidents. Housekeeping is not just about keeping a place clean. It includes ensuring corridors, work areas and floors are neat and tidy and free from slip and trip hazards. Spillages must be cleaned immediately. A safety sign indicating a wet floor must be displayed to prevent any potential accidents by warning people of the hazard and telling them to take extra care.

Waste materials and other fire hazards must be removed from work areas and fire exits and doors must **never** be blocked.

The Safety, Health and Welfare at Work Act 2005 states that workers' duties include the reporting of any defects in the place of work or equipment which may endanger or cause harm. Faulty electrical equipment and wiring must be reported to the person in charge and clearly labelled as being out of order. Trained professionals only must repair the broken or faulty equipment.

Under the Safety, Health and Welfare at Work (Safety Signs) Regulations 1995, safety signs are obligatory in all workplaces to draw attention to objects and situations capable of causing specific hazards (The Health and Safety Authority, 2004). There are many safety signs available for portraying different information, e.g. no smoking signs, fire exits and first-aid points. Safety signs are standardised. Shapes and colours are used to highlight their meaning:

Red =	Stop or prohibition
Yellow =	Caution, possible danger
Green =	No danger, first aid
Blue =	mandatory signs, information
Discs =	mandatory and prohibition signs
Triangle =	warning signs
Squares and rectangles =	emergency and informative signs

Employers must provide information about the safety signs and their meanings to all employees (The Health and Safety Authority, 2004).

According to the Health and Safety Authority, any accidents that occur within the workplace must be recorded in an accident book. The type of record will vary from area to area. The record must be accurate and say exactly what happened. It must be legible, comprehensive and comprehensible. Any witnesses to an accident must complete a witness report. Healthcare workers must check the policy for reporting accidents and incidents at their place of work, so that they understand what is required of them. Doing so will not only help them in their work; it will also demonstrate that safety measures are in place and ensure that any changes needed are identified as quickly as possible.

Fire

Fire prevention is a predominant issue in the safety, health and welfare of everyone working within healthcare settings. All staff must be aware of how to prevent fire and know the procedure for the safe evacuation of patients, visitors and staff if fire does break out. According to the Safety, Health and Welfare at Work Act 2005, all employers must have adequate policies and procedures in place to deal with emergency situations. This means that an emergency plan must be available detailing what should be done in the case of an outbreak of fire. The plan must also include emergency numbers to call and give the location of the assembly point outside the building. Furthermore the Act states that every employer should provide information, training and supervision to ensure the safety, health and welfare of their employees. Employees must be trained in fire safety and, in most healthcare settings, fire training every year is mandatory. All healthcare settings will have different policies, procedures and practices. While employers have a duty to bring these to the notice of employees, all staff must take personal responsibility for ensuring that they are fully aware of these policies, procedures and practices and understand them clearly. Fire exits must be clearly identified, usually with illuminated signs.

FIRE OCCURRENCE

Fire occurs when there is a chemical reaction between three substances: fuel, oxygen and heat. Fuel is something that will burn, is combustible and will ignite. It can be solid, a gas or a chemical. If one or more of the elements is removed, the fire will be extinguished. It is vital that all staff, patients and visitors are aware of how fires can start and how they can be prevented. Smoking outside of designated areas, faulty electrical wiring and equipment, poor housekeeping, heaters, flammable liquids and medical gases are all elements that could contribute directly or indirectly to the start of a fire. (Government Publication, 1996)

FIRE PREVENTION

Fire can be easily prevented if everyone is educated and understands what to do and, just as importantly, what not to do. Trained professionals should check fire extinguishers, electrical equipment and wiring at prescribed intervals. Dates of testing/checking should be clearly shown on equipment. Smoke alarms and sprinkler systems should be fitted and tested frequently in accordance with legal requirements and other recommendations as appropriate, e.g. insurance company requirements. Regular testing of fire alarms and practice evacuations should be carried out to ensure staff members are fully aware of their responsibilities in the event of an outbreak of fire. Smoking should only be permitted in designated areas with correct receptacles provided for the safe disposal of cigarettes.

Good housekeeping will greatly assist in reducing the risk of fire. For example, combustible rubbish should not be left lying around and other potentially dangerous situations should be identified and quickly made safe. Fire doors are installed to prevent or slow the spread of fire and **under no circumstances** should they be prevented from closing, even for a short time. They should **never** be wedged or propped open. Designated fire exits must be kept clear at all times. Obstructing fire exits, however small the obstruction, is very dangerous and can lead to injury and death (Government Publication, 1996). Staff with responsibilities for housekeeping should remain vigilant so that fire-risk assessment becomes second nature to them.

A laissez-faire attitude is dangerous and can, literally, blow up in the face of anyone who adopts it. Remember, fire can kill and preventing one from starting is usually easier than putting one out.

Infection Control

Infection control within both hospitals and community-based healthcare settings is vital in the prevention, acquisition and spread of infection by patients, staff and visitors. Everybody is at risk of infection in healthcare settings. Many sick people with many types of infection in close proximity to each other results in large numbers of micro-organisms coming from different people. There may, for example, be vomiting and diarrhoea and other easily transferred ailments which can quickly spread if precautions are not taken. Healthcare associated infections (HCAI) can be acquired in places such as outpatient clinics, hospitals and nursing homes. An example of an HCAI is methicillin-resistant Staphylococcus aureus or, as it is more commonly known, MRSA. About 10 per cent of all HCAI are MRSA infections (The Health Service Executive, 2007). By their very nature, hospitals carry a great risk of spillages of blood and body fluids which, in turn, carry a great risk of infecting other people. Also, the serious problem of overcrowding remains in many accident and emergency departments, leading to close contact with people carrying infection. The danger of cross-infection, i.e. spreading infection from one person to another, cannot and should not be overestimated. Similarly, the risk to patients who, because of their weakened state, are at their most vulnerable, cannot be stressed too highly and must be recognised by staff and visitors alike. Fortunately there are a number of simple, common-sense steps that must be taken to lower the risks and dangers dramatically.

Infection control is the responsibility of everybody, but staff working within healthcare settings must be aware of their responsibilities to educate patients, visitors and new members of staff. Ultimately, those caring for patients must be aware that the highest possible standard of infection control is an integral aspect of total patient care.

WHAT CAUSES INFECTIONS?

Micro-organisms predominantly cause infection. These are so small they cannot be seen with the naked eye (Dustagheer, Harding & McMahon, 2005). Micro-organisms are everywhere and can survive in many different types of environments, from very hot to very cold temperatures. *Anaerobic* organisms can survive without oxygen, whereas *aerobic* organisms require it to survive (Brooker & Nicol, 2003).

Numerous micro-organisms are to be found in the environment and these have different names according to their shape, size and behaviour. These include the following: viruses, bacteria, Protozoa, fungi and parasites (Dustagheer, Harding &

McMahon, 2005; Brooker & Nicol, 2003).

Such organisms can cause various types of illnesses, some of which can be life threatening. Urinary tract infections (UTIs), infections of wounds, chest infections and MRSA are examples of some of the infections the organisms can cause.

HOW IS INFECTION SPREAD?

Infection can be spread in the following ways:

- *Airborne*: micro-organisms are spread through the air from sneezing, coughing, wound dressings, skin scales and dust from cleaning equipment.
- *Indirect contact* into the blood stream from dirty needles and instruments.
- *Direct contact*: refers to the transfer of micro-organisms following direct contact with an infected patient. Unwashed hands, clothes of staff and aprons and gloves not being changed after treating an infected patient will cause infections to be spread (Brooker & Nicol, 2003).

BARRIERS AGAINST INFECTION

There are many ways in which the spread of infection can be controlled and reduced within a healthcare setting. Effective communication with and education of all staff, visitors and patients is vital to ensure that they are aware of and clearly understand the very real and serious dangers of infections and the common-sense methods of prevention.

Perhaps the most important groups in this respect are staff and visitors. Some patients, for obvious reasons, will be unable to help themselves. Communication can be via spoken word, meetings, leaflets and bright, eye-catching posters. In many healthcare settings posters in each toilet/bathroom indicate the correct hand-washing procedure and remind people of the importance of washing their hands in order to control the spread of infection. Posters should always be maintained in a tidy condition and not allowed to become dog-eared and tatty; otherwise they will soon lose impact. Ideally they should be changed regularly to emphasise their importance and to keep the message fresh in the minds of staff.

A clean environment resulting from sound housekeeping and waste disposal is particularly important, as is the cleaning of equipment, either by sterilisation or disinfection. Correct procedures must be strictly adhered to when isolating patients (*see* 'Isolating Patients' on p. 60). Basic principles of food hygiene must be maintained. Standard precautions must be taken by all staff, visitors and patients in order to minimise the spread of infection in all healthcare settings. Correct hand-washing techniques (see below), the wearing of protective clothing, safe handling and correct disposal of sharps and waste are all crucial factors in ensuring a safe and healthy working environment with minimal risk of the spread of infection (Royal College of Nursing, 2005).

Hand washing

Thorough hand washing is a simple procedure to control infection in healthcare settings. Correct hand-washing techniques used by staff, visitors and patients can help to prevent the acquisition and spread of infection. Hands should be washed with soap before and after direct contact with patients; after contact with bodily fluids; when hands are visibly soiled; when moving from one patient to another; before touching food; after using the toilet; after sneezing or coughing; following the removal of gloves; and after contact with any patient known to have an infectious disease (Gould *et al.*, 1996 in Brooker & Nicol, 2005; Royal College of Nursing, 2005).

Alcohol hand rub is a useful and practical alternative to washing with soap within the healthcare setting. Dispensers should be placed in prominent positions for staff, visitors and patients to use. Simple instructions, together with reasons for using the hand rub, should be prominent alongside the dispensers which must be kept topped up and maintained in sound working order.

Staff should be aware that correct hand preparation can assist greatly in controlling the spread of infection: short, clean fingernails with no nail polish or artificial nails; the avoidance of wristwatches and jewellery (in most places wedding bands are allowed to be worn, but the hand-washing policy in your place of work should always be checked); and cuts covered with a waterproof dressing are all simple, sensible and effective measures to take for the prevention of infection (The Royal College of Nursing, 2005).

Although most people will regard the washing of hands as a simple, straightforward procedure, The National Institute of Clinical Excellence (2003) considered issuing advice on 3 stages to effective hand washing to be necessary:

1. *Preparation*: wet hands under tepid running water before applying liquid soap to all areas of the hands, including underneath a wedding band.
2. *Washing and rinsing*: both hands must be rubbed together for a minimum of 10–15 seconds. Parts of the hands often missed include tips of fingers and thumbs and the areas in-between.
3. *Drying*: hands should be rinsed thoroughly and dried with paper towels, which should then be discarded in the appropriate bin.

Posters demonstrating the correct hand-washing technique should be clearly displayed above sinks in healthcare settings. These act as a reminder to all staff to wash their hands thoroughly.

According to Brooker & Nicol (2005), hot-air dryers are not recommended for hand drying due to the fact that they can blow dirt and dust into the environment.

USING PROTECTIVE CLOTHING

The use of protective clothing is an essential element of infection prevention and control (York, 2002). Protective clothing needs to be worn to prevent contact with bodily fluids or when contact with broken skin or mucous membranes is likely (Wigglesworth, 2003).

Hands must be washed after the removal of and disposal of protective clothing. The removed clothing should be treated as clinical waste and placed into a yellow clinical waste-disposal bag or in accordance with local policy. Learning and understanding clinical waste-disposal policies of each place of work is especially important.

The types of protective clothing used within healthcare settings vary. They can include gloves (non-sterile and sterile), aprons, masks and gowns.

Gloves (non-sterile) are for single use only and should be worn when in direct contact with blood and bodily fluids. Sterile gloves (single-use only) should be worn when carrying out a sterile procedure, for example dressing a wound. Plastic aprons should be used when there is a risk of contaminating staff clothing. They should be single use and disposed of as clinical waste, usually into a yellow clinical waste-disposal bag or in accordance with the policy within your place of work. Masks should be worn where there is a risk of contracting an illness from airborne infections, e.g. tuberculosis, or when there is a risk of splashes from blood or bodily fluids (Brooker & Nicol, 2005).

ISOLATING PATIENTS

If a patient has been confirmed or is suspected of having an infectious disease, e.g. tuberculosis, MRSA or infectious diarrhoea and vomiting, the spread of infection can more easily be controlled by isolating the person in a single room. The type of isolation used for a patient would depend on their condition and their individual needs. How the type of organism can be transmitted, the risk of spread to other patients and staff and the severity of the infection should all be taken into account when isolation is being considered (Brooker & Nicol, 2005).

There are two types of isolation procedures used in healthcare settings:

- Source isolation
- Protective isolation

Source isolation

This type of isolation was previously known as barrier nursing and this expression may still be encountered. The purpose of this is to remove the patient with the infectious disease from other patients and visitors, usually into a single room, thereby reducing the risk of cross-infection and spread of disease (Brooker & Nicol, 2005).

Protective isolation

This type of isolation is often used for patients who are immuno-compromised (Wigglesworth, 2003), meaning that their immune system is not working as well as it should or even that it is not working at all. Treatments for illnesses such as, *inter alia*, cancer and leukaemia, can cause impairment of the immune system. The treatments, therefore, will create a heightened risk that the patient could contract infections far more easily than otherwise might be the case. By being nursed in a single room, the patient is provided with much greater protection from others who could pass on infections to him/her.

It is vital that local policies and procedures relating to isolation measures are readily available for staff to read. In each healthcare setting, procedures and processes may differ, so being aware of and clearly understanding how things are carried out in your place of employment is most important.

WASTE DISPOSAL

The correct disposal of waste in a healthcare setting is vital to ensuring the safety, health and welfare of all staff, patients and visitors. There are many different types of waste found in the healthcare setting and a clear understanding of what is regarded as waste is crucial. There is hazardous waste such as sharps (needles, etc.), soiled waste and infectious waste (items contaminated with body fluids such as blood and incontinence wear from patients with known infectious diseases). Non-risk waste includes waste that is not hazardous to those who come in contact with it. This includes domestic waste such as paper, flowers, hand towels, confidential waste and some types of medical equipment. If staff members have any doubts about hazardous or non-risk waste, they must always seek advice from an experienced colleague before taking disposal action.

The disposal of sharp instruments has remained a concern to healthcare workers for many years. This is because there is a serious risk of injury from the sharps, in particular from needle sticks, with a very real possibility of transmission of blood-borne viruses such as human immunodeficiency virus (HIV) and hepatitis B. As well as needle sticks, sharps include scalpels, broken glass or any other items that may cause a laceration or puncture wound (Royal College of Nursing, 2005). The correct handling and disposal of sharps can greatly reduce the risk of injury. Gloves should always be worn when dealing with sharps. Needles should **never** be recapped or placed into pockets and they should **never** be left lying around for somebody else to dispose of. Whoever used the needle carries the responsibility for its correct disposal. Needles and syringes should always be carried in procedure trays in accordance with local infection-control policy, which should be known and clearly understood. Needles must always be disposed of immediately after use into the designated sharps boxes which should be located close to the area of use.

In most healthcare settings, there are colour-coded bags for waste. Hazardous waste other than sharps are usually disposed of in yellow bags labelled clinical waste. Non-hazardous waste is usually disposed of in black bin-bags. Soiled linen is normally placed in a water-soluble (alginate) bag which is placed directly into a washing machine. The seams of the bag dissolve whilst being washed. This ensures that laundry workers are not at risk from touching the infected linen (Brooker & Nicol, 2005). There may be variations within different healthcare settings, so checking and understanding the local infection-control policy within each place of work is very important to confirm which colour bag to use for hazardous waste. Staff must also check local policies to identify procedures for dealing with spillages.

First Aid

According to the Safety, Health and Welfare at Work (General Application) Regulations 1993 Part IX, employers are obliged to provide first-aid equipment at all places of work (The Health and Safety Authority, 2002). It will depend on the size and function of the workplace as to what type of first-aid equipment is required. Under the regulations, there must also be a trained occupational first aider on site. A first-aid room must also be provided where appropriate (e.g. where there are no other medical facilities such as those in a hospital) and this must be clearly identified. Different first-aid provisions may be required in different places of work. Some places of work are obviously far more hazardous than others, for example building sites and factories. There are other companies that have very large premises and they may need to provide more than one first-aid room so that employees are adequately accommodated.

The aim of first aid is to:
- Preserve life
- Prevent further injury
- Promote recovery (Benson, 2000)

First aid may need to be administered in a life-threatening situation, e.g. when somebody stops breathing or their heart stops. It may equally, and possibly more usually, be required for minor injuries, e.g. cuts and bruises. First aid does not include the administration of drugs or medication (British Red Cross, 1998).

To qualify as a first aider, a person must successfully complete a certified first-aid course. There are various organisations that provide excellent first-aid training. These include, amongst others, the British Red Cross, the Irish Red Cross and the St John

Ambulance charity. By completing a first-aid course, the first aider will be highly trained, examined and regularly re-examined and updated in knowledge and skill.

The first aider may find themselves in a variety of situations where a rapid and rational approach is required. These include: cardiac arrest; shortness of breath; an unconscious patient; minor cuts and bruises; broken limbs; a heart attack; drowning; electric shocks; burns and scalds; eye and ear injuries; road traffic accidents; and poisoning (British Red Cross, 1998).

First-aid kits

It is advisable for everyone to have access to first-aid kits in the home, the car and in the workplace. The contents of a kit in the workplace must conform to legal requirements (St John Ambulance, 2002) which should also be clearly marked and readily accessible. Employees must be aware of the exact location of the first-aid kit and it must be regularly checked and replenished as required.

First-aid kits differ in size and equipment depending on the environment in which they are required. For what it is required is another aspect to consider. For example, someone preparing to go on a trek may well be advised to take a first-aid kit which includes a survival blanket, a whistle and a torch as well as the other basic material. On the other hand, a first-aid kit for an office may only need the basics, which includes:
- Watertight box in which to keep the materials
- Plasters in assorted sizes
- Medium sterile dressings
- Large sterile dressings
- Extra-large sterile dressings
- Sterile eye pads
- Triangular bandages
- Safety pins
- Disposable gloves
- Scissors
- Useful additions
  - Crêpe roller bandages
  - Tweezers
  - Cotton wool
  - Non-alcoholic wound-cleansing wipes
  - Adhesive tape
  - Notepad, pencil and tags
  - For outdoor activities: blanket, survival bag, torch and whistle (St John Ambulance, 2002)

Anyone can come across a first-aid situation at any time – in a shop, in the street, in the workplace or even in a healthcare setting – and this can be a very frightening experience. By completing a recognised first-aid course, the first aider will learn skills to enable them to remain calm and confident in the knowledge that they are acting in the correct way and providing essential primary care.

Manual Handling

According to the Health and Safety Authority (1998), manual handling or minimal lifting should be avoided except in life-threatening situations. Patients, where possible, should be encouraged to move themselves, and equipment assisting patients to do this should be available. However, avoidance of lifting patients is not always possible. It is an inevitable part of working for those who have a responsibility for patient care. Surgery, old age, chronic illnesses and other such ailments can cause immobility and this means that patients may need assistance with moving. Chronic back pain is a common problem encountered by healthcare workers (Health and Safety Authority, 1998). Therefore, in order to minimise the risk to their staff, it is of vital importance that the employer is aware of the manual handling regulations which are contained in the Safety, Health and Welfare at Work (General Application) Regulations, 1993 Part VI (S.I. No.44). Not only must they be aware of the regulations, they must adhere to them. The employer must take all reasonable measures to ensure that manual handling by staff is avoided or, at the very least, kept to the absolute minimum. Within healthcare settings this can, of course, be very difficult. As previously stated, people may be immobile so some degree of assistance must be provided. However, where assistance is required, the employer is expected under the regulations to ensure that manual handling is performed in the safest way possible. A risk assessment – reviewing the environment, the characteristics of the load, the physical effort required and the type of work to be performed – must be completed. Following the risk assessment, employers are obliged to examine how to prevent injury, particularly back injury, to employees (Health and Safety Authority, 2001). This examination will include reviewing the types of equipment, handling aids and training provided for employees to ensure injury is avoided.

Training for staff in the practice of manual handling must be provided in each healthcare setting before they are permitted or expected to move people. Legally, employers have a duty to provide such training in order for staff to avoid injury (Nazarko, 2000). Training must include demonstrations of how people should be assisted correctly with the use of equipment. This helps staff to avoid, as much as possible, manual handling without equipment and to assist people to move themselves, thus encouraging a feeling of independence for the person (Nazarko, 2000). Staff should be taught how to move people who are unable to move themselves, even with assistance, in the safest possible way whilst avoiding injury to themselves, colleagues and the person they are moving. Equipment must be checked on a regular basis and the manufacturer's instructions read and clearly understood. If a member of staff is not entirely clear how a piece of equipment should be used, he/she must seek help and advice from an experienced colleague. Failure to do so could lead to serious injury. If equipment is not working correctly it should be taken out of use and clearly marked as not being in use. If this is not done, harm could be caused to care workers and patients alike (Benson, 2000).

The types of equipment found in healthcare settings to use for safe manual handling include:
- Hoists – electrical and manual
- Sliding sheets/boards/other patient transfer aids
- Wheelchairs with removable armrests
- Walking frames
- Turntables
- Equipment to raise toilet seats and chairs
- Height-adjustable beds

Staff may be reluctant to use the equipment if they are not trained to use it and this may be dangerous for all involved. Therefore the employer must arrange training and insist that all appropriate staff attend. The need for updating and refresher sessions should not be overlooked.

According to the Report of the Advisory Committee on the Health Services Sector to the Health and Safety Authority (2001), employers are required to carry out a risk assessment to identify the risks associated with manual handling. The assessment should include the following points:
- The task
- Individual capacity
- The load
- The environment

The task: The care worker must look at how the handling will affect his/her own body. Will there be twisting of the torso, stooping, stretching upwards, excessive pushing/pulling, excessive carrying, insufficient rest periods, sudden movement of a person and repetitive movements?

Individual capacity: The care worker must be aware of their limitations and of the risks involved in moving and handling. They must be in a position where they can reasonably decline to perform a task if they consider they are unable. The worker should wear loose-fitting clothing, comfortable shoes and receive adequate training. Workers who are pregnant or have health problems may be at more risk than others. The training mentioned above should provide staff with the required self-awareness and confidence to deal with any situation they encounter in an appropriate way.

The load: In relation to manual handling in healthcare, the load referred to is the person requiring assistance. Consideration should be given to the weight of the patient, whether or not they may be cooperative, their health status (physical and psychological), any attachments (e.g. drips, drains or catheters) that may hinder movement and any special-needs aspects that may have to be taken into account, such as broken limbs, wounds, etc.

The environment: A review of the environment is important. This will show if there is sufficient room to carry out the task. It will also indicate the type of flooring and whether or not the heating and lighting are adequate. Additionally it will reveal if the correct equipment is available and in good order to assist in the moving of the patient. Staffing levels are another important factor to consider. Understaffing can, for example, lead to one member of staff trying to move a person when two (or even more) would be essential (The Health and Safety Authority, 2001).

Risk Factors in Relation to Health

Health is a concept that has been widely discussed. According to Clark (1986) in Basford *et al.* (1995), health means there is a balance between the person and his/her environment and focuses upon the physical, social and psychological aspects of a person being in a state of equilibrium.

We all want to live a healthy life. Unfortunately at times we become ill. There are many risk factors that can contribute to ill health (and injury) and a range of social, environmental and economic factors that can influence our decisions. These include poverty, unemployment, lack of access to health services and environmental issues including housing and water (Department of Health and Children, 2000). We make lifestyle choices that can influence our physical and mental health and it is up to the individual to maintain a healthy, balanced lifestyle. Of course there are factors outside our control that can affect our ability to ensure a healthy lifestyle. Age, sex, social class, working and living conditions, income, education, peer-group pressure, mental health and access to information are all factors that can influence our decisions, capacity and capability for living a healthy life (Department of Health and Children, 2000). Becoming ill or injured can seriously disrupt life, restricting daily activities and affecting work, relationships and leisure.

The Department of Health and Children (2000) recognises some of the risk factors that can contribute to ill health as:

- *Smoking*: According to the National Health Promotion Strategy 2000–2005, one in three adults are smokers, with slightly more males than females smoking. Smoking is a known risk factor for heart disease, cancer and strokes.
- *Alcohol*: In moderation alcohol can be enjoyable for many people. However, for some it is an addictive substance which can cause many problems. Accidents, injuries, violence, liver disease, cancers and social problems are all linked with alcohol abuse.
- *Diet*: Good nutrition is vital for the human body to function effectively. It plays a major part in the growth, repair and maintenance of healthy bodies. A balanced, nutritional diet would include some fats, carbohydrates, proteins, water, vitamins and minerals.
- *Drugs*: Drug misuse can cause psychological and physical harm to a person. It can also cause harm to a person's social network, including family, friends and the local community.
- *Exercise*: Taking regular exercise is well known for helping with cardiovascular function, social interaction, weight management and stress reduction.
- *Sexual health*: Unsafe sexual practices can lead to sexually transmitted infections (STIs) and also the human immunodeficiency virus (HIV).
- *Stress*: Stress can be anything that stimulates and motivates. For example, a deadline for an assignment can encourage and, at the same time, increase the level of alertness and output. Life without this stimulus would be dull and boring. However, too much stimulus, e.g. planning a wedding, commencing a new job, moving house, extra work pressures, relationship problems and even going on holiday, could become unpleasant and ultimately damage your health or wellbeing. Too much stress can seriously affect a person's ability to perform effectively or to their maximum potential. (Department of Health and Children, 2000)

Through education and health promotion people can be informed of the dangers of some of the practices they partake in. Every individual is responsible for their own life, and nobody can change anyone unless that person is ready to change themselves. Government policies such as the workplace smoking ban, which came into effect in the Republic of Ireland in March 2004, advertisements, posters, television campaigns, radio programmes, leaflets and information from healthcare professionals can all help to advise and educate people and to emphasise the positive benefits of a healthy lifestyle.

Conclusion

This chapter on health and safety will be useful to those training as HCAs by providing information and also encouragement to treat the subject with the seriousness that it requires. Vitally, healthcare workers must understand the policies and procedures pertaining to safety and health at work. As well as always following these policies and procedures, they will also have to apply large doses of common sense in their day-to-day activities at work.

This chapter has touched on some of the aspects of health and safety which have relevance to a healthcare environment. For other aspects, there are numerous, helpful publications to which reference could be made. A book entitled *Safety, Health and Welfare at Work* by Joseph Kinsella was published by Gill and Macmillan in April 2008. This book addresses relevant issues and particularly health and safety law. Students undertaking courses which include Safety and Health at Work modules will find this book worth reading.

Assignment Guidelines

FETAC Level 5 Safety and Health at Work Module: D20165.

The FETAC Level 5 Safety and Health at Work Module has three assessments and will be based on a range of specific learning outcomes.

Assignments (2) Weighting 60%

There are two assignments to complete as part of this module. The course provider will normally issue briefs for both assignments. As HCAs you will be expected to examine and investigate two aspects of safety and/or health in the workplace.

Exam (1) Weighting 40%

The exam will be theory based to assess learner ability to recall and apply theory and understanding. The duration of the examination will be 1 hour 30 minutes. The format of the examination is:

- *Section A*: Twelve short answer questions (learner required to answer ten).
- *Section B*: Three structured questions (learner required to answer two).

CHAPTER FIVE

COMMUNICATION

Breda Hanrahan

The Communication Process; Communication and Interpersonal Skills; Methods of Communication; Barriers to Effective Communication; Overcoming Communication Barriers; Therapeutic Communication; Learning to Communicate Effectively

Patients are entitled to expect that those who care for them – doctors, nurses and others – will be able to listen, to explain, and to communicate with them. Patients are also entitled to expect that healthcare professionals will be able to communicate effectively with each other. Whatever the circumstances, the need for good communication is constant and is integral to good care.

(Bristol Report, 2001)

Introduction

This chapter will help you, the healthcare assistant, to explore the concept of interpersonal communication in both your personal and working life. It will assist you to identify and to practise a range of communication skills that will enable you to communicate and interact in a meaningful way with your family, co-workers and the people for whom you are caring. It will assist you to review your existing interpersonal and communication skills and help you to make changes where necessary. Effective communication and good interpersonal skills are the tools used to assess situations and allow you to deal with your findings in a competent and sensitive manner, while keeping in mind the wishes of the people involved. According to Covey, communication and interaction will be more effective if you have some prior knowledge of the person with whom you are about to speak. This knowledge will help you in the preparation and the delivery of the message you wish to convey: 'Seek first to understand, then to be understood' (Covey, 1992).

The Communication Process

Communication is the transmission of information, i.e. the sending and receiving of messages. Messages are simultaneously sent and received on two levels: verbally through the use of words, and non-verbally by the behaviours that accompany the words (DeVito, 2004).Verbal communication consists of the words a person uses to speak to another person. Words are used to describe objects and to discuss concepts, to form phrases and sentences that make sense and give meaning to a conversation. Non-verbal communication, or body language as it is sometimes called, includes such behaviours as facial expressions, eye contact, tone of voice and body posture; these behaviours accompany the spoken word. When the non-verbal cues and the spoken message are congruent, the flow of communication is enhanced. As a HCA, whether you work in the person's own home, in a care home or in a hospital, it is necessary for you to be able to understand key terms used in communication theory; terms such as sender, receiver, message, feedback and channels of communication. It is also necessary for you to be able to recognise the kinds of listening skills required in different contexts in your day-to-day activities, e.g. understanding, interpreting and receiving information. Your ability to demonstrate a range of listening behaviours appropriate to the situation will help you and the listener to understand the message being sent, e.g. eye contact, facial expressions, encouragement to the speaker and control over your own responses. It is through the medium of communication that ideas, opinions, feelings and information are shared with others. This sharing of information will help you to improve your interpersonal relationships. Communication requires the participation of both the sender and the receiver; it takes place when the receiver understands the sender's message and responds appropriately. You need to be able to communicate in a meaningful way with the person to whom you are speaking. This means speaking clearly and expressing yourself in a way that will be easily understood by the other person. The way you say something can sometimes have more of an impact than what you actually say. Communication will be enhanced by your ability to interact with other people, and the HCA who possesses effective communication and interpersonal skills will be an asset in the workplace.

Communication and Interpersonal Skills

Interpersonal skills include such things as attitude, empathy, compassion, sensitivity, humour and attentiveness. As a HCA it is necessary to be kindly disposed towards the people in your care, keeping in mind the reason why they need your help. It is important to be sensitive to their needs and feelings, to treat them with courtesy and compassion, and, where appropriate, with humour. A friendly and caring attitude will help you to gain a person's trust and respect, which in turn will facilitate good interpersonal relationships. Attentiveness requires you to focus on the person, listening carefully to what they are saying and keeping eye contact without appearing to stare at them.

Maintain a relaxed position, facing the speaker, nodding your head at appropriate times to show that you are interested in what they are saying.

Effective communication and interpersonal skills will help you as an individual and as a team member to work efficiently for the good of the people in your care.

Methods of Communication

Speaking, using the telephone, texting, emails, facsimile and writing are all forms of verbal communication. Non-verbal communication consists of body language and sign language. All of these methods may be used in your place of work. Some of them you will be very familiar with and some you may not have used at all.

VERBAL COMMUNICATION

The spoken word is necessary to our personal and social development; it remains a central way of delivering messages. You can relay messages via intercom or by telephone, but there are times when it is necessary to speak directly to the person involved, e.g. in problem-solving situations, giving a report or making a request. When you are speaking to another person, direct communication allows you to know exactly what they are thinking and feeling, and, when it is performed correctly, it creates a clear, unambiguous form of communication and reduces the risk of misunderstandings. The process of speaking involves the selection of a topic, collecting information about the topic, organising your thoughts and ideas and eliminating any unnecessary information. You should choose a comfortable, private environment, with the minimum of distractions. It is important for you to adopt a relaxed position, sitting or standing at the same level as your listener, keeping in mind their personal space. Speak directly to the person, keeping eye contact with them, without appearing to stare. Be aware of your own body language and your tone of voice, and speak slowly and distinctly, using words that your listener will understand. Continually check that your message is being heard and understood, by asking appropriate questions. Open-ended questions will give you more descriptive information, while closed questions will give you a 'yes' or 'no' answer. You could ask the person to rephrase or to repeat the message back to you, or you could ask him/her to describe the message using their own words. This will indicate their understanding of the message.

LISTENING

As a HCA you need to be an effective listener. This will enable you to assist people to talk and identify their needs and feelings. You must listen attentively to hear and understand the message they are sending. Listen to how they speak, their choice of words, which words are emphasised; listen to the tone and pitch of the person's voice. It will also be necessary to observe the person's body language to check to see if they are giving the same signals as the spoken words. Are they trying to hide something or are they too anxious or emotional to speak the words needed to convey their message? Have they got the correct words to express their message? Your role as a carer requires you to help them to express as clearly as possible what it is they want to say. You can do this by sensitively asking appropriate questions, or you can prompt them by suggesting a word when they appear to be unable to find the right one. Maintain a relaxed position, facing the speaker; be unhurried and give them time to marshal their thoughts. Encourage them by sayings things like 'go on' or 'I see'. Nod your head at appropriate times to show that you are interested in what they are saying and lend credibility to the speaker. It is also helpful to rephrase what was said, or to repeat the message back to the speaker using different words that have the same meaning.

Telephone

Many times during your working day you will answer the telephone and make telephone calls. While the telephone is a useful way of sending and receiving information, sometime mistakes are made and the messages are misunderstood, often with serious consequences. When you are using the telephone it is very important to speak in a clear, articulate manner. Most hospitals and care homes have criteria or guidelines for using the telephone, and you should become familiar with them. When using the telephone, identify yourself and check that you have the correct person or location and then deliver your message. Check to see if the message was understood by asking them to repeat it back to you. Where appropriate, following telephone conversations make a written record of what was said, the date, the time and your signature. You may need to relate the message to your supervisor, co-workers or the person for whom you are caring. It must be repeated factually as it was stated; not your impression of what you heard. It is also possible to use the telephone to text information. You need to be careful when sending or receiving text messages, particularly if they are related to your work. Text messages are usually relayed in a form of shorthand, which may be misunderstood or taken out of context. If you are tempted to text a work-related message, check it is acceptable and then check the guidelines for doing so.

Electronic mail (e-mail) / Facsimile (fax)

While there are great advantages in using such forms of communication to send and receive information that is urgently required, there may be problems with confidentiality. Therefore it is most important for you to be aware of the rules and guidelines in relation to confidentiality for the use of such equipment in your place of work. In the case of facsimile, transmissions should include a cover on official headed paper from your place of work, stating the confidential nature of the document. When using electronic mail to send information, you need to be extremely careful as it is very easy to make an error and send it to the wrong person or to a large number of people. In most workplaces computer users will have passwords that limit their access to information related to their own particular work.

WRITING

Writing is another important way for you to communicate your thoughts, ideas and feelings to other people. At some stage in our lives most of us will have put something in writing, such as filling out application forms, writing reports or memos of one kind or another. For writing to be an effective form of communication, the communicator will need to have a working knowledge of the writing process, such as how to form a simple sentence and how to spell words used in everyday speech. In the course of your working day you will be required to document important information about the people for whom you are caring. This information needs to be written in a clear and legible style that can be easily read and understood. The contents of the report must be factual, stating what actually happened, not your impression of the event. Thus careful planning is essential to ensure that what you want to write is stated in a clear and unambiguous format. Before putting pen to paper it will be necessary for you to organise your thoughts, what you want to say, to whom you want to say it and what emphasis you want to place on the message. When you have a clear picture in your mind of what you want to say and how you want to say it, you may begin to write, keeping in mind that this report is a legal and confidential document. Your final task in writing a report is to read carefully over its contents and make changes where necessary.

BODY LANGUAGE/NON-VERBAL COMMUNICATION

Social interaction involves numerous forms of non-verbal communication, which is the exchange of information and meaning through facial expressions, gestures and movement of the body. This type of communication is often referred to as body language. Effective communication occurs when there is congruence between the non-verbal and verbal cues given off by the speaker.

Knapp and Hall devised the following list to show how non-verbal messages accompany verbal messages.

- *Accent*: using flashing eyes or hand movements.
- *Complement*: giving quizzical looks, nodding.

- *Contradict*: rolling eyes to demonstrate that the meaning is the opposite of what one is saying.
- *Regulate*: taking a deep breath to demonstrate readiness to speak, using 'and uh' to signal the wish to continue speaking.
- *Repeat*: using non-verbal behaviours to augment the verbal message, such as shrugging after saying 'who knows?'
- *Substitute*: using culturally determined body movements that stand in for words, such as pumping the arm up and down with a closed fist to indicate success (Knapp and Hall, 2002).

Facial expressions communicate emotions such as sadness, hopelessness, despair and fear, and can also indicate joy and happiness. Facial expressions, along with verbal messages, are often used by people to convince the listener to accept what they say is true. Eye contact is a powerful form of non-verbal communication; the direct stare of the person sending the message can convey sincerity and openness or dislike and aversion. Eye contact will help regulate the flow of communication; it can convey concern, warmth and lend credibility to the speaker. Gestures and body posture are commonly used to convey meaning, even when nothing is actually said. Touch is another important form of non-verbal communication and is frequently used by the caring professions. You need to be aware of and respect the person's wishes in relation to touch and their personal space. Some people have an aversion to being touched and like to keep a distance between themselves and other people, while others find touch comforting. Touch, if used incorrectly, can cause mistrust and create barriers to effective communication, but when used correctly it will enhance the communication process. The non-verbal impressions that we give off often indicate that what we say is not exactly what we mean; therefore, it is most important to observe the body language of the person with whom you are communicating and also to be conscious of your own body language: is what you say being contradicted by your non-verbal expressions and actions? Everyday interaction depends on subtle relationships between what we convey with our faces and bodies and what we say with the words we use. Listening to what people say and observing their body language will let you know if there is a conflict between the verbal and the non-verbal cues or if there is harmony, where both are sending similar messages.

Sign language

Sign language is used to communicate with people who are unable to hear and/or speak. It is a specialised form of communication and unless you work with people who cannot hear you are unlikely to be able to communicate through sign language. Sometimes people who cannot hear are admitted to care homes or hospitals or may need care in their own home; therefore, it is important that your place of work would have the name, address and telephone number of a person who can perform sign language.

Barriers to Effective Communication

This includes such things as an unsuitable environment, lack of privacy and constant interruptions, all of which can cause communication breakdown. This occurs when the sender's message does not get through to the receiver or the receiver misunderstands the sender's message. A breakdown in the communication process will cause messages to be misunderstood and inappropriate actions to be taken, sometimes with serious consequences. Therefore it is most important for you to be aware of and understand the potential sources of communication barriers and to make a conscious effort to avoid them, thus reducing the risk of distorting the meaning of your message. Your choice of words and language (encoding) will also influence the person's understanding of the message you are sending. Words have different meanings which in themselves may distort the meaning of the communication and the language you use will need to be understood by your listeners. Ignoring non-verbal cues or misreading body language will also lead you to misunderstand the speaker's intention. Another type of communication barrier is selective hearing. In this situation the person chooses to hear only what he wishes to hear; he will filter out things that he finds too distressing or painful and things that might require him to make life changes. Distorted perception occurs when the person's life experiences affect their perception of what was said. Anxiety can interfere with the communication process and may reduce the ability of the person to hear and understand what is being said. Physical difficulties such as impaired vision or hearing will cause problems with receiving and understanding messages. Barriers to effective communication can also be caused by psychological problems, which can have an adverse effect on the communication process; e.g. a person with learning difficulties will find it hard to comprehend some of the things that are being said which, in turn, will interfere with his ability to understand the message. As this is not a comprehensive discussion on barriers to effective communication, I would advise a more detailed study, using the suggested reading at the end of the book.

Overcoming Communication Barriers

Knowing the common barriers to effective communication is the first step to minimising their impact on the communication process. If possible, have a quiet, private environment with comfortable seating and good lighting and keep the distractions to a minimum. If a room is not available you will have to improvise and find a quiet area that is private. It will be necessary for you to assess the ability of the person to hear and understand verbal communication. Assess them for physical problems such as impaired vision or hearing or speech impediments; check for psychological difficulties, e.g. if they are depressed or anxious, or if they have a learning disability.

If you discover that the person has a communication problem, it will be necessary to devise a plan with the person involved that will help in overcoming communication barriers. Seek clarity by asking open-ended questions which will require the speaker to describe the problem or his feelings in relation to it. Consider the words you are using and the structure of the sentence. Unfamiliar words and long, complicated sentences may confuse your listener, especially if the person is anxious or worried about their state of health. You should speak in a clear, concise, articulate manner. If the listener appears to be having difficulty in understanding your message you could repeat the same words again or you could rephrase what you said. Seek regular feedback, which will indicate where the problem is and allow you to deal with it in an appropriate manner. Show concern, be courteous and unhurried. Sit or stand at the level of your listener, keep eye contact but do not stare. Be aware of your own body language and observe your listener's non-verbal cues: are they relaxed or are they showing signs of stress which could impede communication flow?

Therapeutic Communication

Therapeutic communication describes a meaningful relationship between the person being cared for and the healthcare provider. You can facilitate therapeutic communication by maintaining patient-centred listening, suppressing your prejudices and establishing a trusting relationship with them. This will help to create a therapeutic environment where the person will feel it is safe to disclose and discuss personal and health-related issues. The person may need to be reassured that privacy and confidentiality will be maintained. You can do this by letting them know of the confidentiality clause in your contract of employment. To encourage the person to talk, sit close to them at their level, being careful not invade their personal space as it might cause tension and anxiety which in turn would interfere with their ability to relax and discuss their problems. To gain a better understanding of what the person means, observe their verbal and non-verbal cues. These cues can prompt you to ask questions that will help the person to voice their worries and concerns connected to the problem. Let them see that you are genuinely interested in them and in what they are discussing with you. Empathise with them and let them see this by touching them if permitted. Touch, where allowed, can comfort and help the person to relax, but first you must check to see if it is acceptable to them. Observe for cues that will indicate if touch is desirable. You could place your hand on the person's shoulder and observe their reaction, or you could ask them about touching, e.g. 'Would it comfort you if I put my arm around your shoulder?' Always adhere to their wishes. There are many therapeutic communication techniques you can use to interact with patients; your choice of technique will be guided by the person's ability to communicate verbally. You could help the person open up to you by asking them if there is something they would like to talk about, where they would like to begin, then encourage them by prompting, e.g. 'Go on . . .', 'And then. . .' Help the person to put their concerns in context by saying, 'Was that before or after . . .?' 'What seemed to lead up to . . .?', thereby helping to identify the cause and the pattern of their problem. Restate or rephrase what was said. This will help to clarify some issues. Give feedback and let them know how they are doing. Observe the person's face: does it express anger or sadness? You could say 'You look sad' or 'Are you angry?'. This will help them to be aware of their feelings and encourage them to speak about them. During the discussion it might be helpful to sit in silence with the patient, allowing time for them to think and reflect on their problem. This will give them the opportunity to organise their thoughts before speaking about their concerns. Ask for feedback by saying, 'Does this word mean . . .?' or 'I don't follow . . .'. This will help clarify the message. Encourage the patient to discuss their problem in greater detail, by saying, 'Tell me more about your worries and concerns in relation to this problem; what do you think would help to solve it?' Close the interaction by summarising the main points of the discussion and plan with the person how to proceed. Would further discussion help or is expert help needed to solve the problem?

The above discussion on therapeutic communication will help you to interact in a therapeutic manner with people of all ages and in all circumstances. You can use it as a template or guide and adapt it to suit the particular circumstances of the person with whom you are interacting. For example, when communicating with an older person keep in mind that they are likely to have physical barriers to effective communication such as impaired vision or hearing or speech difficulties as a result of a stroke. They may be confused or depressed, which could be permanent or may be short term due to the person being in an unfamiliar environment and once the person becomes orientated to their surroundings the confusion and depression will disappear. Regardless of the age of the person or what problems they appear to have, it is essential to assess their ability to communicate effectively before involving them in therapeutic communication sessions. The assessment must reflect the person's spirituality and religious beliefs which will influence their thoughts and feelings in relation to how they communicate in general. Spirituality concerns the person's beliefs about life, illness, death and their relationship to the universe. According to Andrews & Boyle, religion is an organised system of beliefs about one or more all-powerful, all-knowing forces that govern the universe (Andrews & Boyle, 2003).

Religion and spirituality are subjective and, as such, can be emotive subjects. Being aware of your own religious and spiritual beliefs will help you to be objective and non-judgmental when caring for people with different beliefs and values to yours. Following the assessment of the person, and having chosen appropriate therapeutic communication techniques to assist them with their concerns and worries, you and the patient will plan how to conduct the therapeutic communication session. When communicating therapeutically with children and young people, their parents' or guardians' consent is necessary. In most situations involving children and young people, parents or guardians will be present and will be involved in the interaction. Therefore it is necessary for you to be aware that some or all of the communication may be transmitted by the parent to the child. You must ensure that its meaning is not lost or changed in the transmission. Further reading will be suggested at the end of this book.

Learning to Communicate Effectively

One approach might be for you to reflect on your personal style of communication: how you speak, your tone of voice, the words you use and your body language.

Reflection is the process of reviewing an experience in order to describe, analyse and evaluate it to inform your learning about practice (Reid, 1993).

Reflecting on practice involves thinking about your action and describing it verbally by taping it, putting it in writing or discussing it with your supervisor. You should reflect on what you thought, how you felt and the action you took. Through looking back at the experience you can think about the attitudes, thoughts and feelings you had before the event: have these attitudes, thoughts and feelings changed as a result of the experience? Negative feelings about an experience can prevent you reflecting in an appropriate manner on your actions. Such feelings as disappointment, unrealistic expectations of your self and a feeling that you could have performed better will affect your ability to reflect in a meaningful way on your experience; hence the need to deal with your negative thoughts and re-evaluate your experience. Only if you are willing to make changes, using the insights gained from reflecting on your practice, will reflection help you to develop good communication skills and become an effective communicator.

Keeping a journal and logging your experiences on a regular basis will help in monitoring your progress. Document your thoughts, feelings and attitudes about your actions, along with the feelings of those involved and how they responded and reacted to your actions: include any feedback from your supervisor and co-workers. When writing in your journal you need to be aware of confidential and legal issues. You must not document anything that would identify the people or conditions relating to them. Legally your journal can be requested and used in court proceedings; therefore you should think carefully before you write and if you are unsure you should seek the advice of your supervisor. To improve how you speak and to help you to feel confident about speaking in public, you could tape yourself speaking, then critically listen to a playback. Listen to the tone and pitch of your voice, its fluency or hesitancy and your breathing pattern. Be aware of the sound of your voice, the words you use and how you pronounce them. You could ask a trusted friend or family member to critique your voice on tape. Listen to other people speaking, especially people you consider to be good speakers; compare and contrast the way you speak with way they speak. If necessary you could attend public-speaking classes or societies.

Assignment Guidelines

FETAC LEVEL 5 COMMUNICATIONS MODULE: G20001

Communications is a compulsory module for all FETAC major awards at Level 5. This chapter will be a support tool for those undertaking the course, but it is hoped that you will continue to use it in your day-to-day activities. You are required to carry out two assignments to complete the module.

Collection of work: 50% weighting

This assignment requires you to compile a collection of your own work that demonstrates evidence of communication skills covered in the course, such as writing skills. You will be expected to produce a short, structured report and a minimum of three other pieces of writing, demonstrating your ability to communicate effectively in writing. You will also be expected to produce evidence of your ability to communicate using technology, e.g. mobile phone or email.

Skills demonstration: 50% weighting

You will be expected to make a presentation of approximately five to ten minutes' duration demonstrating your listening and speaking skills. You will also demonstrate your ability to communicate without using words, for example by designing an image poster, or demonstrate your non-verbal skills by making a non-verbal presentation such as mime or dance.

CHAPTER SIX

WORK EXPERIENCE

Blathnaid Connolly

Globalisation and Demographics; Employment Opportunities; Skills Audit; Work Experience; Setting Goals; Writing your CV and Application Forms; Interview Skills; Getting a Job; Employment and Equality Legislation in Ireland

Introduction

This chapter focuses on the world of work and where you, as an individual, fit into it. The process of seeking work, applying and being interviewed for a job, can be laborious and time consuming, but ultimately rewarding. It is important to be adequately prepared. The energy and effort you put into your preparation will contribute to your success. The way we work has changed. Globalisation has meant there is movement of trade, technology and people across the world. The Irish economy has grown substantially in the last five to ten years; this has created a demand for adaptable, flexible and skilled personnel. An increasingly ageing population has meant that there is a need for skilled practitioners in all areas of healthcare services. Both the public and private healthcare sector must respond to market demands. Therefore employers seek people who are committed and display qualities that will contribute to the whole organisation's success. Many employers often consider personal skills such as the ability to communicate, use initiative and work within a team more important than technical skills that can be taught. To get a good job you must compete with others who may have similar or more experience than you, in addition to having vocational education and skills. Perhaps you are undertaking further study to gain a qualification. It is important, therefore, to identify what you can bring to any job and to recognise your true worth.

Globalisation and Demographics

Globalisation may be a term you have heard in many contexts. From an economic perspective it refers to the growth and development of trade and business across the world. There are many multinational corporations whose brand and product are recognised globally. The explosion in communication technology has created a global media that can be accessed by most parts of the world. The Internet and air travel makes movement and communication easier, for consumers and businesses alike. There are as many supporters of globalisation as there are critics. Those in favour feel that it creates economic prosperity and stability in those countries involved. However, critics argue that this is detrimental to the local businesses, economies and culture, particularly of smaller countries who find it hard to compete (*Globalisation Guide*, 2006). It is not only businesses that travel, but people; the same factors are attractive to a skilled labour force that will travel to find work and prosperity. Ireland has seen much immigration, particularly from other European countries. The largest population increase since statistics have been collated was in 2005–2006, with over a 100,000 increase in the population (Central Statistics Office, 2006). This enriches the cultural tapestry of Irish society. It also means the workforce is bringing skills and knowledge from other communities and cultures. However, it can present challenges in terms of language, understanding and the need for tolerance and acceptance. The economy has seen unprecedented growth over the last ten years. There are many factors which contribute to this: industry in Ireland has moved away from agriculture towards technology with tax incentives for technology companies (O'Connell & Russell, 2005); a large portion of the population is young and in employment; and there has been growth in the number of females joining and returning to the workforce. This has increased the number of households where both parents are working, and has increased the prosperity of individuals and families (O'Connell & Russell, 2005). The growth of employment is predicted to continue and a skilled, educated labour force will be needed (Lunn *et al.*, 2007).

Employment Opportunities

The role and function of the HCA is currently under review. The government is currently reviewing it in light of the provision of the Further Education and Training Council (FETAC) Award for HCAs within the Health Service Executive (HSE). With additional knowledge and training it is expected that the HCA role will develop with expanding responsibilities. You may be currently working in the healthcare sector or considering it as a future career option. Alternatively you may be undertaking work experience in this area with the hope of future employment. There are many opportunities for the right candidate. Other chapters will have discussed the role of the HCA, how they function within the workplace and what skills and qualities are required to be competent in the caring role. In this chapter we will discuss your suitability to the role, and provide guidelines on how you can prepare yourself for the workplace. HCAs can be found in many areas of the healthcare sector. Therefore it is important to have an idea of what your particular area of interest is. You may already be working in your ideal job, but if not write in the diagram below all the workplaces in which you are aware that healthcare assistants can be found (see figure 6.1 below).

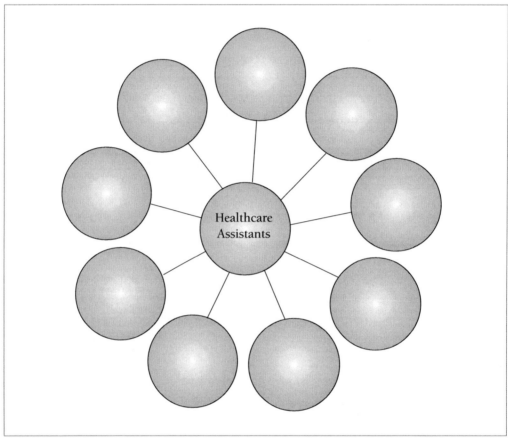

Figure 6.1

You can add additional circles if you wish. Next think of which area would suit you best. You may have to ask yourself some questions. Which area sounds the most interesting/challenging? What age group of people would I prefer to care for? What hours can I work? Do I have reliable transportation/childcare, etc? It is important to consider these factors because when you find the right job you need to be sure it is suitable to your lifestyle and your personality.

Skills Audit

There are many ways to assess your current level of knowledge and skill. You may wish to apply for a position but feel that you have not got relevant or enough experience in that particular area. However, you must remember that many of the duties and responsibilities that you will be expected to undertake can be learned on the job. The experience and knowledge you have gained in another career can also be transferred to this current position. Likewise you may wish to develop in your current workplace. Taking on additional responsibilities or moving to a different area of speciality will mean learning new skills and gaining more knowledge. Carrying out a skills audit gives you the opportunity firstly to identify your current skills and then to look at what areas you need to develop further. This will help you when you are writing your curriculum vitae (CV) or completing an application form. Firstly spend a couple of minutes thinking about all the things you can do, or have done in the past. Consider your professional life, work experience, voluntary work undertaken and your personal life, hobbies and domestic activities. You may be very proficient on the computer or the captain of a local club, secretary in your church, etc. If you are a recent school-leaver, consider the activities you were involved in, e.g. the debating society, drama society, school prefect. All these positions carry responsibility and require organisational ability. Make a list of everything you can think of and put it into categories under the following headings: (1) technical and practical skills and (2) interpersonal and personal skills. Making a list of your personal qualities and interpersonal skills can often be much more difficult because it means you must think about the type of person you are and how you interact with others. Try and be as honest as possible and ask your friends and family to help you. Examples of different skills have been listed below, but remember you are talking about yourself; we are all different with our own individual qualities. Therefore you do not need to match everything on the list.

TECHNICAL AND PRACTICAL SKILLS

- Computer skills
- Managing money/budgeting
- Writing letters
- Design/art skills
- Making things
- Problem-solving

INTERPERSONAL AND PERSONAL SKILLS

- Willing to learn
- Able to listen
- Able to take responsibility
- Confident
- Able to communicate

- Assertive
- Able to lead and be led
- Sense of humour
- Ability to organise
- Ability to speak in front of a group

By carrying out this exercise you will have realised that you have many different skills and qualities, that when combined make you the person you are. It is important to remember that all skills are transferable; as a HCA many of these skills and attributes are extremely useful and, in fact, are often the reason you have moved into the area of care. Next think of all the skills and qualities that you consider essential to the HCA role. Make a list of the attributes you consider in order of importance. For example, it is essential for someone to be caring and kind. However, they may not be good at organising their time, but this is a skill that they can learn on the job. Again some examples have been listed below.

SKILLS AND QUALITIES NEEDED TO BE A HEALTHCARE ASSISTANT

- Punctuality
- Reliability
- Good team worker
- Friendly
- Patient
- Empathetic
- Good communicator
- Honesty
- Willingness to learn
- Add additional qualities and skills you feel are needed to the list

Finally, take some time to consider what skills and qualities you need to develop to become more effective in your role, or in any position you hope to fill in the future. How will you go about developing yourself? Do you need to undertake further training or education? Do you require work experience? Do you need to improve your team-working or communication skills? You may need to seek the advice of your colleagues, friends or employer to identify areas of potential growth. If you are currently undertaking further training or education, much of what you learn through the course materials and the assignments can be applied to your personal development or growth, particularly in the area of personal reflection. This allows you to examine your interactions with the people around you, the communication skills that you use and areas that require improvement for personal and professional growth.

Work Experience

Many educational and training courses require you to gain some experience in an area relevant to your chosen subject. 'Work experience is a planned experiential learning activity and is an integral part of an educational process' (FETAC, 2001). This is very beneficial to you and can also be beneficial to the employer. The purpose of work experience is to provide the learner with an insight into what that area of work involves. This includes the tasks and responsibilities required of the role, the services provided by the organisation and the way in which it is structured, including the people employed there. Work experience does not mean you do not participate in the tasks and activities taking place. Quite the opposite: the more involved you become the more you will learn from the experience. The employer will provide you with guidance on what is expected of you during your work experience. It is very important to follow these guidelines so that no harm comes to you, your colleagues or your clients. There are many learners undertaking further study in the area of healthcare; therefore there is a lot of competition for work-experience placements. For the employer it can be very valuable to get to know someone in this way; they can observe them and identify their suitability to the role. Therefore you should look at your work experience as potential for future employment in addition to a valuable learning experience. Managers will expect the same qualities from work-experience students as they do from their staff. Therefore it is important to be punctual and stay for the duration of your shift as agreed. You must also, where appropriate, dress neatly and have a tidy appearance. Displaying a willingness to learn and respecting the experience and knowledge of the team with which you are working will make your experience more meaningful and will impress the employer.

Setting Goals

Regardless of the length of time spent on work placement, it is important to set objectives or goals that you wish to achieve. This is also an essential component of the assignment for the FETAC Level 5 Work Experience module. The assignment will be discussed at the end of the chapter; however, a large part of it involves the evaluation of what you learned during the experience and the contribution you made during your time there. Setting learning goals will assist you in this process. You may also be required to carry out some practical assessments for other FETAC Level 5 modules; you could make this part of your learning goals. Refer back to your skills audit. Identifying personal, interpersonal or practical skills you hope to develop will provide you with guidelines for goal setting.

Please see the example below:

TECHNICAL/PRACTICAL SKILLS

- Bed-making
- Assisting patients with feeding, toileting, cleansing and dressing

PERSONAL AND INTERPERSONAL SKILLS

- Using my initiative
- Asking questions to assist learning
- Developing listening skills
- Improving communication

INCREASE KNOWLEDGE

- Health and safety policies
- Learning about the organisation
- Learning the roles and responsibilities of different team members
- Considering my future career aspirations

Finally it is important to discuss your goals with the employer. Being well prepared creates a good impression. Also they need to be aware of any assessments or written reports they will be expected to complete. Explain this to them early in your placement; they are busy people and may get annoyed if they are expected to fill out unfamiliar paperwork at short notice.

Writing your CV and Application Forms

APPLYING FOR A JOB

Now that you have spent some time evaluating your current knowledge and skills, you need to be able present yourself to potential employers. The first step is your letter of application and curriculum vitae (CV). The quality of your presentation will create a lasting impression on those reading it. If your presentation is poor, it is unlikely you will get to the interview stage. When advertised, many job positions will state what the employer considers to be the 'essential' requirements of the role, whereas skills may be described as 'desirable'. You must read this carefully. The essential skills and knowledge are the minimum requirement for doing the job; if your skill set does not match this, it is unlikely you will be considered for the position. If no specific criterion exists for the position, there is no reason why you cannot apply. It depends on your level of enthusiasm, your commitment and your ability to adapt to a new situation.

LETTER OF APPLICATION

This must accompany your CV. Try to make it concise and to the point. It should contain your address, the date and the potential employer's name and address. If you know their name, address it to them, e.g. 'Dear Mrs Mason'. Do not use their first name; it is too familiar. If you do not know their name, address it 'Dear Sir/Madam'. The purpose of the letter is to express an interest in the position advertised and outline your suitability for the role. You do not need to give them your employment history, that is what your CV is for, but you could write a brief outline of your current role and responsibilities and explain why you think you are suitable for the position. When ending the letter you must sign off 'Yours sincerely' if you have addressed them by name or 'Yours faithfully' in the case of 'Dear Sir/Madam'.

Preferably the letter should be typed, but it is acceptable in written form if it is very clear and easy to read. The employer may have received many applications for the same position; if they find it too difficult to look at an application they will simply discard it. The following example of a letter is for guidance only.

EXAMPLE OF LETTER OF APPLICATION

24 Old Road
Old Town
County Carlow

24 September 2008

Mrs Mason
The Nursing Home
New Road
County Carlow

Dear Mrs Mason,

I wish to apply for the position of senior healthcare assistant as advertised in the *Carlow Tribune* on 21 September 2008.

I am currently working as a healthcare assistant in a thirty-bed nursing home. I have been in this role for five years. I have gained extensive experience in all areas of caregiving and enjoy my job very much.

Recently I received my FETAC Level 5 Award in Healthcare Support. I found the course to be both rewarding and challenging and it has helped me develop the skills and abilities necessary to take on a more senior position. I have enclosed a copy of my recent curriculum vitae.

I look forward to hearing from you.

Yours sincerely,

Mary Jones
Enc. [*this signifies that you have enclosed documents with the letter*]

C U R R I C U L U M   V I T A E   (C V)

This provides a summarised history of your education, qualifications and work experience to date. It must be typed and should be no more than two pages in length if possible. Although many organisations use application forms, it is still important to have an up-to-date CV. It should be laid out in neat order, starting with personal information and progressing to educational qualifications. Your employment history is then detailed, starting with the most recent and going backwards. This should also include a brief outline of each role and your duties or responsibilities. Try and make this specific to the post for which you are applying as the employer is considering your suitability for the current position they have available. Use concise points rather than long sentences. You then include your interests and hobbies; again this can be brief. For those with only a short employment history or school-leavers, you could write a concise piece on your future career ambitions, including any work experience or voluntary work you have undertaken. You must provide information about references; these are people from whom your potential employer will seek information about your suitability for the job and personal characteristics. Normally these will include your most recent manager, past employers or college tutors, etc. It is acceptable to write that references will be provided on request and provide them after the interview if asked to do so. This is also useful if you are keeping your CV on file, as your referees may change. Remember to ask permission for a reference before providing their details. Do not lie or over exaggerate the information you provide; the chances are you will get caught out. Also do not try to hide information; you may have gaps of time where you were minding children, looking after sick relatives, etc. Try to promote these experiences as something that can contribute to the skills and qualities required for the position available. Spend time creating your CV and always keep a copy. Try to have it on computer file or disc so it can be updated as required.

EXAMPLE OF CV LAYOUT

Personal Details:
Name/address/contact details, including email.

Education and Training:
Include details of school/college, dates of attendance, details of educational qualifications.

Work Experience (employment history):
Start from current or most recent position and go backwards in date order.

Achievements:
Refer to your skills audit (see p. 82). There may be achievements here that will display factors such as leadership or communication skills.

Hobbies and Interests:
It is important to demonstrate that you have a life outside of work. This can also display personal attributes and qualities, such as being a team player or having an interest in your community.

References:
On Request.

APPLICATION FORMS

Many organisations now use application forms as part of their recruitment process. Your CV will be very useful when completing it. Always make a couple of copies so you can practise filling them out. You will find that the application form is designed in a particular way; the employer has done this so they can retrieve the information they require and it is also kept on your file if you are employed. You can use most of the information found in your CV. In addition to this you may be asked about your work-permit status and your PPS number, information you would not normally put on your CV. The application form is a confidential document, and a statement of this is normally found on the form. Again do not lie or exaggerate the information you provide. Be concise; there may not be a lot of room so you want to get the important information across to the reader. Make sure you fill it out neatly; you may be able to get a copy online that you can type out. Remember to read all the instructions carefully and follow them. If it asks you to write in CAPITAL/BLOCK letters, you must do so. Write in black pen so that it can be photocopied. If there is a space for you to provide additional information about yourself, do not ignore this; it may be your only opportunity to discuss your personal qualities and your suitability for the role. When you are happy with all the information you are providing, write it out carefully and neatly on a fresh application form. Remember to keep copies of your application form and your CV. Familiarise yourself with the content as it will be the main source of information at interview.

Interview Skills

Congratulations, you have reached the interview stage. It is natural to be nervous before an interview. In fact nerves are important as they can help you to perform well. However, if you are overly anxious you may forget what you want to say. Therefore preparation is everything. Firstly read the job advertisement carefully to obtain as much information as possible and do some research on the organisation to find out their size, number of employees, what their main function is, etc. Gather as much information as you can about the position. If a job description is available, try to get a copy of it so you can be prepared to answer and ask relevant questions. Make a list of questions you think you will be asked, and prepare general answers to them. It is likely you will be asked about yourself, your previous work experience, education and qualifications and your aspirations for the future. Think of your qualities and what you can bring to the role; you are sure to be asked about this. It may feel silly, but practise talking out loud in front of friends or to a mirror. It will help you to remember the information you want to get across. Prepare questions you would like to ask. You could ask about the role itself or opportunities for future training and development. This is not the appropriate time to ask about money, holidays or terms and conditions, as it may give an inaccurate impression of your intentions. Asking questions shows that you are serious and interested in the position. Finally make sure you are appropriately dressed: opt for a smart suit, with a tie for men. Accessories are not essential and make-up should be minimal for women. Be clear on the location of the interview, what mode of transport you will use, and allow plenty of time to get there in case of delays. It is better to be early than on time, and being late is unacceptable. Despite your nerves, when you greet the interviewer smile and offer a firm handshake. Wait to be shown to your seat, and allow the interviewer to introduce themselves before starting to speak. When answering questions, try to keep a calm, controlled voice; expand on your answers unless the question requires a specific 'yes' or 'no' answer. You must listen carefully to the questions so that you are sure you are answering them correctly, and keep to the point. Remember your CV or application form outlines your skills and experience. The interview is your opportunity to show who you are; be enthusiastic and let your personality shine through. Body language is very important; make eye contact and remember to smile. When the interview is coming to an end remember to thank the interviewer and allow them to tell you when future contact will be made. Afterwards congratulate yourself for getting through it; even if you are unsuccessful it is a valuable experience and your technique will improve with practise.

Getting a Job

It is a great feeling when you are successful as a result of your hard work and achievements. Working provides social contact, challenges, opportunities and financial reward. When you start your new job there will be a lot to learn; initially this can be an anxious time, but it gets easier as you become familiar with your surroundings, your duties and your colleagues. Your employer has expectations of how you will perform. They will want you to be punctual, work hard and fulfil the duties required of you and be committed and loyal to the people around you. You should inform yourself as much as possible about the organisation. The team of people you work with will come from varied backgrounds and have many different skills; get to know them so that you have a deeper understanding of how they work and what their responsibilities are. This will improve communication and understanding. Be helpful and willing to take on new challenges, but follow the guidance of the senior qualified staff as they have overall responsibility for your work. Good luck!

Equality and Employment Legislation in Ireland

As an employee you have various rights and responsibilities in the workplace, as does your employer. The law governing working practices in Ireland is detailed under various acts of legislation. The Safety, Health and Welfare at Work Act (2005), already discussed in Chapter 4, outlines the duties of both the employer and the employee in relation to safety and health in the workplace. The Equality Act (2004) determines that no person should be discriminated against on the grounds of age, race, gender, sexual orientation, family status, disability or as a member of the Travelling community. Discrimination means where one person is treated less favourably than another. The Equality Authority, formed in 1999, has the responsibility of ensuring that discrimination does not occur in the workplace. This Act, which was updated from its first introduction, is also concerned with sexual harassment which, in any form, is unlawful (Equality Authority, 2007). A contract of work is where an individual agrees with another person to execute any work or service for that person, and it can be oral or written. The employer must provide the employee with a written statement of terms and condition within two months of employment (Terms of Employment (Information) Act, 1994). There is a minimum wage in place to which all experienced adult workers are entitled. The term 'experienced adult worker' describes any employee who has been employed in any two years since turning eighteen. A person on work experience is not entitled to pay, but someone in training may be subject to lower than the minimum wage whilst undergoing their training (National Minimum Wage Act, 2000).

The maximum working week is forty-eight hours per week; however, this is calculated over a four-, six- or twelve-month period, depending on the circumstances. This is particularly relevant to those working in seasonal employment. Every employee is entitled to a fifteen-minute break after working for four and a half hours, or thirty minutes after six continuous hours, but the employee is not entitled to payment for breaks (Organisation of Working Time Act, 1997). Payment for compassionate leave, sick leave or overtime is not statutory, which means that you are not automatically entitled to it. However, each employee is entitled to a payslip with every payment. Notice of termination of employment should be reasonable and detailed in the aforementioned terms and conditions. There are exceptions to all of these Acts and there are many other Acts covering different aspects of employment that will be relevant to different people at different times in their lives. The Data Protection Act 1988 and the Data Protection (Amendment) Act 2003 ensure that all citizens' information should be treated confidentially and not used inappropriately. This means that all information that you hear about your clients must be treated confidentially and with respect. You should never discuss your clients outside of the workplace, and during work information about clients should only be discussed in the appropriate circumstances (Source: Citizens Information).

Assignment Guidelines

The FETAC Level 5 Work Experience module incorporates three modes: work placement, work practice and work-based learning. It is a compulsory module for all FETAC major awards at Level 5.

WORK PLACEMENT

This is for those students who attend work experience in a suitable area, normally arranged by their course provider. The object of the work experience is to gain 'hands-on' experience of their chosen area of study; they are supervised by the manager in the workplace.

WORK PRACTICE

A structured programme of learning is organised and assessed by the course tutors and coordinators in the classroom or college environment.

WORK-BASED LEARNING

This is relevant to learners who are undertaking a FETAC programme related to their current role or a previous one.

There is a portfolio of work required. Guidelines for this are devised by the course provider. It is then compiled by the learner during their work experience. There are differences in the portfolio depending on which mode is applicable to the learner.

The following are included:

Learner record

This is similar to other learner records you have to complete for other modules. However, it is primarily concerned with how you plan and prepare for the work experience, what you learned whilst there and evaluation of the impact the experience had on you. Much of the activities in this chapter, such as carrying out a skills audit, setting learning goals, compiling your CV and letter of application, will assist you in the development of your learner record.

Skills demonstration

You will be assessed in the workplace by your manager/supervisor as you carry out a variety of skills-based activities. Again your learning goals may help you in planning this activity.

Assignment

Your course provider devises the brief for this. The content is concerned with the industry/sector in which you are gaining work experience, i.e. the health services sector. You will need to identify different individuals working in the sector and what their role involves. You will then need to assess the future employment and career opportunities within the sector.

CHAPTER SEVEN

CARE OF THE OLDER PERSON

Mary Vernon

The Ageing Process; The Positive and Negative Effects that Ageing has on the Individual; The Benefits of Preparing for Retirement; Promotion of Healthy Ageing; Development of Positive Attitudes Towards the Older Person; Needs of the Older Person when their Health is Compromised; The Role of the Healthcare Assistant; Promotion of Healthcare Issues in Care Settings; Needs of the Older Person with Chronic Illness; Needs of the Older Person with Cognitive Impairment and Physical Disabilities; Nutritional Needs Including Special Diets and Specific Needs of Older Residents; Care Settings and Services for the Older Person

Introduction

It is not possible to cover in detail all aspects of ageing and related care skills in this chapter. However, we will endeavour to give an overview of some of the most important issues and aspects of care skills associated with the older person.

It is important to remember that ageing is a normal process and we age from the day we are born. There are many definitions of older years which will vary within different cultures, and among individuals. The definition for healthy ageing that I have chosen is taken from *Healthy Ageing, A Challenge for Europe Project*, June 2007. It defines healthy ageing as the process of optimising opportunities for physical, social and mental health to enable older people to take an active part in society without discrimination, and to enjoy an independent life of good quality. This project was co-funded by the EU Commission and aims to promote healthy ageing among people aged 50 years and over. It also states that one-third of Europe's population will be 60 years and over by 2025, with a significant increase in the number of people aged 80 years and over. Longevity in Ireland is 72 years for men and 75 years for women. A report from the Economic and Social Research Institute (ERSI) showed that 11 per cent of the Irish population are over 65 years. The demographic characteristics between European countries will vary due to historical and cultural differences.

It is also interesting that the Irish government have at last acknowledged the importance of the older person by the appointment of a Minister of State for Older People in 2007. The care of the older person in Ireland in the past, and generally in the present, was and is that of a homogenous population. The future care will include other nationalities, not just from Europe but from all over the globe.

The Ageing Process

Ageing does not start at 65 years; it is not a sudden event. It begins at birth and continues until death. The physical changes of ageing become more obvious during middle age: hair greys, wrinkles appear and strength declines. Ageing is individualistic; people do not age at the same rate. Ageing is influenced by one's state of mind and outlook on life. The person who feels old will often look and act old. A well-known saying is true: 'We are as old as we feel.' There are many factors that affect ageing, such as heredity, environmental, lifestyle, physical health and mental health. Heredity describes the characteristics that we inherit from our parents and ancestors. In some families there is a long lifespan and parents and grandparents have lived to be very old. Environment plays an important part in the ageing process. Conditions such as air, water, noise levels where we live and work have a major influence on healthy living. People live longer in an environment that has clean air, clean water and low noise levels. Lifestyle not only affects how long we live but also how we live (quality of life). Smoking and the abuse of alcohol and drugs shorten life. Emotional and social activities may contribute to a destructive lifestyle. Stress and the ability to cope with stress have an effect on our lifespan. Good nutrition, regular exercise, adequate sleep, relaxation and good social interaction contribute to a healthy lifestyle. Developing this kind of lifestyle helps to lengthen the lifespan. People who are in good health do not age as quickly. They remain more active and involved in meaningful activities, thereby feeling more useful and independent.

It is not possible in this chapter to discuss the structure and functions of all the body systems.

The human body is a combination of nine systems:

1 The skin and appendages (fingernails, toenails, hair and sweat glands)
2 The Musculoskeletal system
3 The Respiratory system
4 The Circulatory system
5 The Digestive system
6 The Urinary system
7 The Nervous system
8 The Endocrine system
9 The Reproductive system

1. THE SKIN AND APPENDAGES

No system in the body works independently; therefore a change in one system will affect the others. The first signs of ageing are often seen in the skin and hair. The skin gets thin and more fragile, loses its elasticity and wrinkles appear. It becomes more easily damaged. The fatty tissue between skin and bone gets thinner, which means less protection and insulation – this may cause older people to complain of feeling cold. Less sensitivity in the nerve endings may cause inability to identify sensations.

2. THE MUSCULOSKELETAL SYSTEM

Changes due to ageing in the musculoskeletal system may have an effect on daily living tasks such as dressing, washing, toileting, walking, eating, etc. Brittle bones increase the risk of fractures. Stiff joints reduce mobility, which has an effect on daily living activity. Disturbance of balance and instability increase the risk of accidents. Changes related to ageing in the musculoskeletal system may interfere with the ability of older people to care for themselves and remain independent, and increase the risk of injury.

3. THE RESPIRATORY SYSTEM

Any changes in the respiratory system would have an effect on the older person's ability to breathe, which would further restrict the level of physical activity. A decrease in the elasticity of the lungs increases the risk of lung infections. These changes will reduce the amount of oxygen that is absorbed into the body, affecting all other systems.

4. THE CIRCULATORY SYSTEM

Changes in the circulatory system are the cause of both physical and mental disabilities in the older person. The movement of blood throughout the body is slower. The heart muscle weakens, which means the heart pumps with less force. The heart works harder to keep the blood moving, but is less effective. This results in a decrease in blood flow. Blood vessels that harden and lose their elasticity become narrow. Fatty deposits may block the narrow vessels.

5. THE DIGESTIVE SYSTEM

The digestive system has many changes that occur with ageing. A decrease in saliva and in the sensitivity of taste buds causes a decrease in appetite. Older people often have difficulty chewing and swallowing. Because of shrinking of the gums, dentures become a problem which also affects chewing. The absorption of essential minerals and vitamins is reduced. Peristalsis (wave-like contractions of the intestines that move the contents of the digestive system) is slower, which may lead to constipation. Digestive juices are reduced, which makes it harder for older people to digest food. Because of these changes digestion is less efficient in older people.

6. THE URINARY SYSTEM

There is a decrease in kidney filtration because of the reduction in the number of functioning nephrons (small cells responsible for the filtering of the blood). This can cause a build-up of waste products and toxins in the body. Loss of elasticity in the muscles of the bladder means the bladder holds less urine and for shorter periods of time. The muscle that keeps urine in the bladder weakens and the urine leaks involuntarily, causing varying degrees of incontinence.

7. THE NERVOUS SYSTEM

The numbers of neurons (cells) decrease with ageing. Slower circulation also affects the nervous system. These changes delay the transmission of messages, causing slower responses and reflexes. Nerve endings in the skin become less sensitive, thus reducing the sense of touch. Older people are often more forgetful, especially in relation to short-term memory. Older people who remain active and involved with others are less likely to experience a decline in memory, intelligence and awareness. The five senses are sight, hearing, smell, taste and touch. Ageing affects the special senses in various ways. Many older people experience difficulty reading small print and many need glasses to correct their vision. Changes of the nerve fibres and receptors in the ear may cause hearing loss and the sense of balance may be affected. The accuracy of smell may be reduced and taste becomes less distinct. Sensitivity of touch may be altered. These changes may interfere with the older person's ability to communicate, protect themselves and generally enjoy life.

8. THE ENDOCRINE SYSTEM

Changes of ageing in the endocrine system affect the level of hormones in the body. There is a decrease in oestrogen and progesterone, and insulin becomes less effective. Changes in the hormone levels decrease the endocrine system's ability to regulate body activities.

Decrease in oestrogen results in a loss of calcium, causing bones to become more brittle.

9. THE REPRODUCTIVE SYSTEM

As well as causing problems associated with the endocrine system, a decrease of oestrogen after menopause causes thinning and drying of the vaginal wall. In men, there is a decrease in sperm, the prostate gland enlarges and hardens, in turn causing pressure on the urinary system. Regardless of changes in the reproductive system, sexual needs continue for both men and women.

It is important to remember that all body systems are interdependent; a change in one body system will affect the others.

The Positive and Negative Effects that Ageing has on the Individual

The negative effects are often associated with fear of the possible limitations that the ageing process may bring. Retirement from work and its effect, i.e. loss of job status, social withdrawal, reduced income, loss of self-esteem and changes in the daily routine, may have negative effects, e.g. being at home all day with husband, wife, partner or alone. Isolation due to lack of mobility, illness or changes in financial status may have negative effects on the individual.

The positive effects associated with ageing are about doing what we want to do rather than what we have to do, having time for ourselves and our newfound freedom. There is the enjoyment of travel and the development of hobbies and pastimes, time for involvement with grandchildren and lifelong learning by continuing our education into our older years.

Keeping a balance between our physical, emotional, intellectual, spiritual and social wellbeing will improve and maintain our positive outlook on life.

The Benefits of Preparing for Retirement

The ethos of retiring at 65 years from a permanent, pensionable job is changing. In Ireland, with improvement in the economy and the 'Celtic Tiger', the old approach to retirement has changed. We now have early retirement schemes, changes in pensions and voluntary redundancies. Retirement is an important stage in life. Some people look forward to retirement, but others avoid all preparations. When preparing, we need to consider all aspects of our lives: the physical, emotional, financial and social. Some employers offer pre-retirement courses and it is important that the husband, wife or partner also attends these courses. The contents of these courses cover financial matters, including entitlements, legal issues, health, leisure activities and relationships. Financial security is often a cause of worry because a reduction in income is certain for most people when they retire. Therefore, preparation for a change in lifestyle is necessary. Planning for financial security after retirement should start as early as possible, but this does not seem important to people in their twenties or thirties. Many people are living into their eighties and nineties, which is a great achievement but it may also cause problems for pension schemes, healthcare and the social-welfare system.

Remaining physically active in retirement has a broader dimension; it not only keeps us healthy but also has a social and emotional benefit. Emotional problems associated with retirement often involve a change in status. Instead of being a healthcare assistant, nurse or teacher, we have an 'ex' added onto the title, e.g. ex-healthcare assistant, ex-nurse. For most people this is a major life event. Relationships are often affected, as before retirement the focus in life was job and career. Husbands, wives and partners have made a life of their own with activities that do not involve their 'other half', so in some instances they grow apart. It takes time and patience to develop the relationship again and form a balance that is acceptable to both.

When we move out of the formal work situation, our social contacts generally change and it is often necessary to build a new social life. This may be achieved by involvement in leisure activities such as golf, bowling, walking, outings, social gatherings and joining clubs and associations, e.g. Active Retirement Association. We all have talents and skills, but don't have time to develop them. With retirement we have time to explore our creativity in the various art forms. Another way of becoming involved in the community is to volunteer your services, e.g. to youth clubs, sport clubs, day-care centres or local church. Helping others improves our self-esteem and gives a sense of purpose to our lives.

Continuing our education will keep us intellectually stimulated and broaden our interests. Keeping abreast of current affairs will help to broaden our thinking and improve our intellectual wellbeing.

Relationships with children/grandchildren can be a source of satisfaction and delight in retirement. Grandparents may also become childminders; this may start off as beneficial to all concerned, but the retiree may find the demands and energy drain too high.

The word 'retirement' means to go away or withdraw from something, generally our formal work. It does not mean we have to withdraw from living during a period of life that can be the most enjoyable and fulfilling.

Promotion of Healthy Ageing

Promotion of healthy ageing is seen as one of the major challenges for Europe. A continuously growing older population will have a significant impact on the economies, healthcare, social development, welfare and general wellbeing in Ireland and Europe. Therefore there is a need to increase our knowledge about how to promote good health among older people, and the quality of life in the later stages of life. It has been proven that staying active keeps your body younger and it is never too late to start. Activity prevents stiffness of joints, prevents osteoporosis and gives the immune system a boost, thereby preventing colds and infections. It helps in the prevention of heart disease and diabetes. Activity helps us to keep mentally alert, cheers us up, prevents depression and renews energy levels.

Planning for healthy ageing promotion should involve older people by working with the various organisations such as Age and Opportunity, which is the national organisation, and voluntary organisations such as Senior Citizens Parliament, Age Action Ireland, The Active Retirement Association, and Go for Life. These organisations have become involved in promoting active participation of older people in all aspects of life. Access to information regarding healthy ageing must be made available to all levels in the community, including people from different educational backgrounds, ethnic and cultural minorities, and those living in urban and rural areas.

Promotion of healthy ageing should focus on all aspects life and living, be it physical, emotional, intellectual, social or spiritual. The publication of *Healthy Ageing – A Challenge for Europe* in April 2007 and *The Irish Longitudinal Study on Ageing* (TILDA), coordinated from Trinity College Dublin, will inspire future developments of health promotion for all older people.

Promotion of healthy ageing in care settings is sometimes neglected. The following are areas that should be given priority:

• Encourage choice of a good, nutritious diet
• Build exercise into the normal daily routine
• Value and encourage active participation in activities
• Emphasise and develop personal skills and strengths
• Encourage independence
• Educate and provide information on health promotion.

Development of Positive Attitudes towards the Older Person

Attitudes towards the older person are in the process of change. In June 2007 we had 'Say No to Ageism Week', which highlighted areas where age discrimination was reported to the Equality Authority. Discrimination on grounds of age is illegal by law in both employment and in the delivery of goods and services. Combating ageism takes time because it means changing attitudes which, in some cases, have developed from an early age. Changing of structures and laws is also necessary, e.g. access to employment, promotion, use of mandatory retirement-age limits and voluntary redundancy packages. Ageist attitudes tend to put all people of a certain age together with preconceived ideas of how they should behave, and create stereotypes, e.g. older people are associated with sickness and disability. People can become ill when old, as do other age groups. The person is not ill because they are left with limited function. The often-used statement,

'What can you expect at your age?' shows a stereotyping attitude.

It is also necessary for the older person to change their own attitudes to ageing by not adopting certain roles and behaviours which society imposes on them.

How do we improve attitudes to ageing? Primarily by looking at our own attitudes and through education. Age and Opportunity's Agewise programme was established to educate and inform the public about ageism and discrimination. Their workshops help people with their own attitudes as well as planning for change in their workplaces and practices.

Needs of the Older Person when their Health is Compromised

One of the main fears in the older years is that of illness and dependency. For the older person to become ill is often perceived by them as a crisis. The severity of the illness, whether it is acute or chronic, will determine the level of distress and upset. Reassurance plays a major part when caring for an older person, and developing trust and confidence will contribute to their recovery. The older person is liable to all forms of illness, just like people of any age. As we get older some diseases and conditions become more prevalent, e.g. arthritis, diabetes, stroke, coronary heart disease, cancer, high blood pressure, cataracts, dementia, Alzheimer's and respiratory conditions. Some of these conditions become chronic. Any of these conditions will have an effect on normal body function, behaviour, dependence levels and mental ability. It is not possible in this chapter to cover in detail all aspects of care for the various conditions. All clients require an assessment of needs on an individualised basis and encouragement of independence where appropriate. Respect and dignity must be maintained during all aspects of care.

The following needs are guidelines which may be used for assessment of all clients, regardless of illness:

- Physical needs include hygiene, dressing, elimination, eating and drinking, safety requirements and mobilisation.
- Social needs may include provision of activities, accommodating the pursuit of leisure activities, encouraging visits of family and friends, outings. Personal choice must be taken into consideration.
- Emotional needs include good communications, providing time to listen to worries, fears and anxieties, encouraging respect, self-esteem and dignity and perhaps acting as an advocate for a client.
- Recreational needs are often connected to social needs, but may include access to music sessions, bingo, reminiscence therapy, arts and crafts and outings to shows, cinema, parks and shops.
- Environmental factors include assessment of risk to the client, awareness of the client, ensuring a comfortable and pleasant environment is maintained, and

awareness of factors in the environment that could compromise safety.
- Spiritual needs include facilitating religious beliefs and practices.

It is important to keep the client informed about their illness/condition. This will help the client to cope better and be involved in any discussion regarding their treatment and rehabilitation.

The Role of the Healthcare Assistant

The role of the HCA is to assist in the delivery of care under the supervision of a registered nurse. The duties of HCAs may vary depending on the care facility in which they work. Many of the duties involve assisting the clients with the activities of daily living. Each facility provides a job description, which will vary from one facility to another.

The HCA provides basic care. They assist with and/or provide care in the following areas:
- Personal care and hygiene
- Bathing
- Mouth care
- Skincare
- Hair care
- Dressing
- Elimination needs, e.g. going to the bathroom, use of a commode and bedpans
- Nutritional needs
- Assistance when necessary with eating and drinking
- Mobilising needs
- Exercise positioning
- Maintaining a safe environment, e.g. infection control
- Ensuring the environment is conducive to sleep and rest, i.e. noise levels from radios and televisions are at an acceptable level.

Communication and interpersonal interaction is an essential part of a carer's role. Other duties may vary depending on the job description:
- Bed-making
- Cleaning bed tables, lockers, etc.
- Caring for equipment
- Measuring input and output
- Collecting specimens
- Observing, reporting and recording information
- Assisting with admission, transfer and discharge of clients.

Education, training and governmental guidelines will determine the appropriate responsibilities.

Promotion of Healthcare Issues in Care Settings

Health promotion is the action taken to encourage or help people to maintain or improve their health and general wellbeing. As with healthy ageing, it is necessary to take a holistic view and look at the physical, mental, emotional, social, spiritual and environmental health of the individual. Promotion of health in the care setting is very individualistic as there are many different diseases and disabilities. Some general guidelines for health promotion are:

- Health education classes
- Keeping active, both physically and mentally
- Choice of food if possible
- Importance of exercise, appropriate diet and calorie intake
- What is an ideal weight and how to maintain it
- Keep in touch with family and friends
- Outings and various activities
- Support and development of hobbies, interests and pastimes
- Health screening and medical checkups, e.g. blood-pressure and blood-glucose monitoring, breast screening, vision and dental check-up (even if the person wears dentures)
- Encouraging independence, even in a limited way
- Promoting good hygiene practices to prevent infection, e.g. providing facilities for hand washing

The layout of the care facility should be conducive to social contact and mobilisation. It should be welcoming, clean, well lit and ventilated. Good communication is essential as it is not always easy to explain to older clients/residents the importance of diets, exercise, etc. It takes time and patience. It is important to remember that health and wellbeing are not just related to physical health. Health promotion is for clients, staff and visitors.

Are you a positive role model?

Needs of the Older Person with Chronic Illness

A chronic illness is an illness that usually begins slowly and lasts for a long time, in some cases a lifetime. Most chronic illnesses are not curable, but they can be controlled by treatment. Correct treatment and care are necessary to prevent complications. Examples of chronic illnesses are arthritis, chronic respiratory conditions, confusion, dementia, Alzheimer's, diabetes, Parkinson's disease, multiple sclerosis, stroke and coronary artery disease. When caring for clients with chronic illness or conditions, the basic principles of care are the same as that of any client, with specific emphasis on the disability or limitation associated with the illness.

One of the most common chronic illnesses that needs assistance, both while in the community and healthcare setting, is arthritis. Arthritis is a chronic disease that causes inflammation of the joints, which are red, swollen, hot and painful. The two most common types of arthritis are osteoarthritis and rheumatoid arthritis. Osteoarthritis is mostly associated with older people and can lead to loss of function and independence.

The role of the HCA in caring for a patient with arthritis is to assist with the activities of daily living as necessary. Encourage the client to do as much as possible for themselves. Allow them to move at their own pace. Position and support the body, maintaining good body alignment. Support and encourage activity. Provide assistive equipment when needed, e.g. special cutlery and crockery for eating and drinking. Assist the client to move safely, i.e. no slippery surfaces, safe position of furniture and equipment. Support and assist with exercise as ordered by the physiotherapist.

Chronic obstructive pulmonary disease is used to describe many of the conditions that affect the respiratory system. It is a progressive condition in which the airway is obstructed. The client will have dyspnoea (difficult breathing), cough, wheezing and lack of energy. Breathing difficulties will limit the client's mobility and activities. They will need assistance with most of the activities of daily living. Special needs include positioning to help easier breathing, either upright in the bed with a backrest support of pillows or in an armchair. Frequent mouth care is necessary due to dryness as a result of mouth breathing and when oxygen is used.

Encourage frequent rest periods and observe for signs of fatigue. Fluid intake and adequate nutrients are also important. If the client has a productive cough, observe the standard precautions for contact with body fluids. Be aware of safety precautions if oxygen is in use. Provide emotional support for client's fear and anxiety. Observe any change in the breathing pattern or colour of the client and report promptly.

Cardiovascular accident (CVA) is the medical term for what is commonly called stroke. The type of disability depends on the area of the brain involved and the amount of damage to the area. A stroke in one side of the brain will affect the opposite side of the body. The client's speech, swallowing, movement, digestion and elimination may also be affected, depending on the area of the stroke. Paralysis, the inability to move a part of the body, is common. A client who has had a stroke can have many problems affecting any of the body systems.

To establish a care plan for clients with stroke it is necessary to do an assessment. The needs will depend on the level of disability. Position the client in correct body alignment and provide support for affected limbs. Introduce rehabilitation training in daily activities and provide assistive equipment as needed. Allow time for activities and do not rush the client. Provide a calm environment and have patience and understanding. Feed the client if necessary on the unaffected side. When assisting with dressing, put clothes on the affected side first. Remove clothes from the unaffected side first. Involve the client's family in rehabilitation and remind them that recovery takes time. If there is any impairment of the sensory systems, observe non-verbal communication and any other means of communication. Depending on the level of disability, the client may need assistance with elimination. Frustration and depression often occur with clients with stroke. It is important that any change in the client's mood is reported. Depression can affect the rehabilitation process.

It is not possible within the limits of a chapter to deal with all of the chronic conditions, but it is hoped the examples given will help you understand the importance of the assessment of the needs of the individual clients. By doing this the priorities of care will be established.

Needs of the Older Person with Cognitive Impairment and Physical Disabilities

The most common problems of the sensory system involve sight and hearing impairment (speech impairment is less common). The majority of older people are affected to some degree by one or both of these impairments. This can result in communication difficulty and loss of independence.

IMPAIRED VISION

People of all ages may have vision problems. The majority of vision problems are corrected by wearing glasses and contact lens. As we get older there may be some degenerative changes which will affect vision. There are two eye conditions that are frequently seen in older people: cataracts and glaucoma. These conditions are treatable if diagnosed in time. Regardless of the cause, impaired vision in older people causes anxiety and fear. Adaptation to change is more difficult for the older person. Encouraging independence, retaining dignity and maintaining self-respect are essential for every individual. Visual impairments are variable; therefore the needs will depend on the extent of the impairment. All activities of daily living may be affected. Establish safety in the environment by ensuring the client knows the position of the call bell bedside their locker and radio. As they may be able to distinguish between light and dark, they need to know where the light switch is. Give directions to the dining room, day room, bathrooms, etc. by easy-to-touch landmarks, wall rails, pictures, change of floor surface, e.g. tiles to carpet, and awareness of hazards in their path such as Hoovers, trolleys, flexes and commodes. If anything needs to be moved, always put it back in the same place.

Communication is of special importance for the visually impaired. When approaching always introduce yourself and say what you are going to do. Address the individual by name as they cannot see that you are talking to them, and always say when you are leaving. Speak clearly and normally as there is no need to shout as many visually impaired people have good hearing. Touch is also an aspect of communication – a pat on the back or a squeeze of the hand can be very reassuring and comforting. At mealtimes special help will be needed, but first ask if they need assistance. A frequently used aid is the clock face to describe the plate of food and keep to the same system. Use a plate with an upturned rim to help prevent the food from sliding off the plate. Impaired vision can cause feelings of isolation as well as the fear of loss of independence. Remember that sometimes the greatest need is for companionship.

IMPAIRED HEARING

Hearing problems can range from being slightly hard of hearing to total deafness. One or both ears may be affected. The hearing loss may involve inability to hear low, medium or high-pitched sounds or a combination. Like the other senses, hearing becomes less acute as we get older. There is little that can be done to prevent this. In some cases hearing aids may be of some help. They should only be used following consultation with a specialist. Models and types of hearing aids vary and it is important that the client is given adequate instruction for their use. The hearing aid should be checked regularly to ensure it is in working order and that it is switched on when needed. Batteries should be checked regularly, the volume adjusted to suit the individual and ensure there is no whistle sound. Hearing aids are not suitable for nerve deafness.

When speaking to a person with hearing difficulties, face the person, speak normally and clearly and do not shout. Lighting should be good to aid lip-reading. When speaking, control the background noise, e.g. radio and TV. Use non-verbal communication to try and convey your message if necessary. Other aids and equipment are available, e.g. special light flashes for the doorbell and headphones for the TV. Their telephone can be fitted with an amplifier to the earpiece, the ring tone may have an extra bell added or a light flashes when the phone rings. These aids will enhance the life of the older person with hearing loss. Patience and sensitivity are necessary in the care of people with hearing loss.

COGNITIVE IMPAIRMENT

Cognitive impairment or memory loss occurs with normal ageing. Memorisation becomes more difficult: dates, names and numbers are often forgotten. Whilst remembering and recalling may take time, the ability to think clearly is not affected. Recent memory loss is more commonly affected. In the majority of cases forgetfulness is not severe and does not get worse with time. The use of diaries, calendars and lists will help in improving memory. This type of memory loss does not indicate that a client has dementia, confusion or Alzheimer's disease. Patience and understanding are needed when caring for clients with memory loss.

PHYSICAL DISABILITY

Physical disability is usually the result of some chronic condition. It can include a variety of problems such as restricted mobility, impaired vision or hearing, altered body function, or a combination of any of the above. The needs of a client with physical disability have already been discussed in relation to care of clients with chronic illness and with sensory impairment.

Assessment of the individual is required to establish their needs and the assistance necessary with the activities of daily living. As well as caring for their physical needs, it is important to treat the whole person, which includes emotional, psychological, social, sexual and spiritual needs. With physical disabilities it is important to commence rehabilitation early; stress what they can do, not what they cannot do. Encourage activity as it helps prevent complications (e.g. pressure sores), improves circulation, digestion, elimination and mobility.

Rehabilitation will encourage independence, increase mental alertness and self-esteem. The environment should be conducive to the health and safety of the individual. Encourage family participation in the rehabilitation process. The team approach is essential. Work together with other members of the healthcare team – nurses, physiotherapist and speech therapist – to ensure the continuity of care. Encourage the correct use of aids to assist with mobility, e.g. wheelchair, walking sticks and walking frames. The choice of equipment will depend on the special needs of the client. Education and training are necessary for the clients and staff in the use of all equipment. Praise even the smallest effort. Positive attitudes such as sensitivity, empathy and patience will contribute to positive outcomes for the client. Relearning takes time, so don't rush and watch for signs of fatigue or exhaustion. Encourage rest and relaxation.

Rehabilitation should be continued for clients who are in long-term care. The aim is to assist a client to achieve and maintain function at the highest possible level of independence.

DEMENTIA IN THE OLDER PERSON

Dementia is defined as irreversible deterioration of mental functioning resulting from organic brain disease (*Dictionary of Nursing*, Churchill Livingstone's 1st Edition, 2002).

The causes of dementia include Alzheimer's disease, multiple infarcts (mini strokes), trauma, infectious toxins, arteriosclerosis and age-related atrophy. An example of infection is Creutzfeldt-Jakob disease (CJD). Being old does not mean having dementia. Only approximately 5 per cent of 65-year-olds have dementia. This rises to 20 per cent over the age of 80. Clients with dementia are unable to think clearly or remember accurately.

In the early stages of dementia severe memory loss may be observed by family and friends. There will be changes in personality and deterioration in personal care, impaired reasoning ability and disorientation. Other symptoms include wandering, aggression and eating problems. Incontinence of urine and faeces may also be a problem.

As a result of a combination of these problems, people with dementia may be admitted to nursing homes, continuing care wards and residential homes.

Like other diseases and conditions, the needs of a client with dementia will depend on the individual. As a HCA you have an important role to play in caring for people with dementia. It is one of the most challenging areas of your work as it is both physically and emotionally demanding.

There is no typical client with dementia. Some are agitated, angry and aggressive, while others are quiet and gentle. One of the common problems associated with dementia is that communication skills decrease. As a result, socialisation becomes difficult and in the later stages it is impossible. Don't assume that because communication is difficult it is useless. Each time you communicate, introduce yourself and speak your name. Repeat the client's name during the conversation. Use all senses when communicating and observe for non-verbal messages. Use smiles to reduce the client's fears. Visual aids such as word cards may be helpful (*see* Chapter 5 for more detailed guidelines regarding communication).

Changes in behaviour may be as a result of some physical discomfort or emotional disturbance. Physical discomfort may be due to incontinence, hunger, constipation or pain. Emotional concerns may be fear, anxiety, depression, boredom or loneliness. Environmental factors may also contribute to behavioural problems, such as noise, glare, over stimulation, uncomfortable temperature, change of location and crowds. Not enough rest or sleep, or too much activity, may also affect behaviour. Maintain a calm environment, reduce stimulation, turn down radios and TVs, and move away from crowds or noisy individuals. Separate clients who have conflict with each other. Keep the client safe and protect them from injury. Identify hazards that may result in trips or falls. Use signs for wet floors and spills. Encourage the clients to wear suitable shoes rather than slippers, as these do not provide good support. Avoid the use of rugs. Make sure the edges of floor coverings are not worn out. Wires and flexes need to be safely placed and not under carpets. Try to keep floor areas free from clutter. Clients who continue to smoke should be brought to the designated area. It is advisable that cigarettes should not be accessible to patients with dementia; this is for the safety of all clients and staff.

Security

Some clients with dementia are disorientated and confused and are inclined to wander. The locking of external doors, especially at night, is essential. Many care facilities now have secure units which are self-contained and the door is locked using a security code. Other institutions have various types of alarms fitted to external doors. External doors are also a means of escape so people should also be able to exit, especially in the event of fire. Monitoring devices for clients are also available but are not in general use. Activities of daily living are affected as the client's condition deteriorates. They lose the ability to wash, dress, eat and drink or use the toilet. The abilities of a client with dementia may decline to the extent where they need help with all aspects of living.

Family

Be supportive to family members and encourage visits. Look for suggestions from the family regarding the care plan. Encourage the family to bring photo albums and mementos of the past; this sometimes helps the client to remember. Stress the importance for family members to communicate with each other.

There are certain qualities that are necessary to help you care for clients with dementia. They include tolerance, patience, humour, sensitivity and respect. Knowledge of how dementia affects clients will help you understand the changes in behaviour. Working with clients and helping them with activities that give them pleasure or make them smile will really make a difference and is its own reward.

Nutritional Needs Including Special Diets and Specific Needs of Older Residents

Food is one of the most basic physical needs. It is necessary to create energy for all bodily functions. Proper nutrition means a well-balanced diet that contains all the elements for physical and emotional health. Food contains nutrients that are necessary for metabolism; most foods contain more than one nutrient. The three major nutrients are protein, fat and carbohydrates. Foods are measured in calories. A calorie is a unit of heat produced as the body burns food. Some foods have more calories than others. Fluid is as essential to life as food and oxygen. We need one-and-a-half litres of fluids (8–9 cups) daily, and this is especially important for older people living in warm, centrally heated environments and during warm weather. Older people are inclined to cut down on drinks because of the fear of incontinence and not wanting to get up at night.

The nutritional requirements of older people will vary between individuals. Most older people require fewer calories because of a decrease in metabolism and physical activity. Requirements for all other nutrients remain the same. There are some factors that affect nutrition in older people:

- Difficulty chewing and swallowing and dental problems
- Impaired mobility
- Illness, disease and medications
- Dementia, confusion and emotional problems
- Decreased appetite
- Personal preferences, cultural and religious practices.

Most care facilities serve three meals a day. For clients with good appetites it may be difficult to get the nutrition required. Extra nourishing snacks between meals may benefit these clients. For clients with malnutrition or at risk of malnutrition, consultation with the dietician and catering staff is essential. Addition of extra nourishment to the client's meals can be accomplished through easily digested protein, e.g. soups and stews. Supplementary drinks, of which there are many available, can be taken hot or cold. These will add extra calories, proteins, vitamins and minerals to the diet.

The HCA is in a position at mealtimes to observe the clients. Observe the amount of food that is served and the amount left on the plate after the meal. Observe any difficulties with chewing and swallowing. Any problems should be reported to the nurse in charge. Weighing the clients on a regular basis will help to detect weight loss, which should be reported to the nurse in charge who will inform the doctor.

There are no special foods recommended for older people. It is advised to serve traditional dishes with which the clients may be more familiar. Where possible, the preference of the client must be taken into consideration. Be aware of any cultural or religious preferences.

Some clients are on special diets ordered by the doctor. The dietician will give direction to the catering staff. In some instances the dietician will do a direct assessment of the client's needs. An example of the most common special diet associated with older people is a diabetic diet. The purpose of this diet is to maintain the correct blood sugar level and prevent complications. The diabetic diet is simply a low-sugar diet. If the client is on insulin, meals and snacks should be served on time. Encourage the client to eat all of the food that is served. Report to the nurse in charge if the client is not eating. Examples of other diets are low-fat/low-cholesterol, high-fibre, clear-fluids and liquid diets. Mealtimes are the highlight of the day for many clients, meeting emotional and social needs as well as physical needs. Many religious festivals are associated with special foods, e.g. Christmas dinner.

Encourage clients to eat in the dining room. It should be clean and bright, well ventilated and uncluttered to aid access for clients with mobility difficulties. Different tablecloths, flowers on the table or table decorations will make a difference to the client's enjoyment of the food.

Preparation of the clients for meals is an important part of mealtimes. Offer toileting before meals. Assist with hand washing and oral care. Check that they have their dentures, glasses and hearing aid. Help the client to be seated and positioned comfortably. Check that the correct diet is being served. Arrange the meal in front of the client. Assist as needed by cutting up meat, buttering bread and opening cartons. Provide special aids as necessary, e.g. food guard, built-up handles, easy-grip mugs, etc. Food should be served at the correct temperature, hot food hot, cold food cold. Some clients will need to be fed due to physical or psychological disability. Make sure the client is positioned correctly, sitting up as straight as possible. Communicate what you are going to do. Sit down so that you are at eye level, and lower the bedside rail if the client is in bed. Tell them what food you have on the tray; if possible let them see the food. Encourage the client to help where possible, e.g. holding the bread. Only half fill the spoon and feed with the tip of the spoon. Check that liquids are not too hot. Alternate food and liquids. If the client is paralysed on one side, feed on the unaffected side. Talk to the client even if there is no response. Wipe the client's mouth as necessary. Make sure the client is clean and comfortable after the meal. Report and record any problems. Record fluid intake where necessary.

Remember that mealtimes meet physical, social and emotional needs. Food is necessary to create energy for all bodily functions. Proper nutrition means a well-balanced diet that contains all the nutrients – protein, fat, carbohydrate, vitamins and minerals – necessary for physical and emotional health.

Care Settings and Services for the Older Person

The aim of any of the services is to keep the client independent for as long as possible and remain in their own homes or sheltered housing in the community. Accessing information regarding the various services is sometimes difficult. In recent years information brochures and books became more widely available from libraries and citizen information centres.

The type of service needs will depend on the illness/disability as well as the individual circumstances. Social services may also be necessary. The core of all health services is the general practitioner (GP).Key personnel in the community services are the public health nurses, HCAs and home help. Facilities that support clients living at home are day centres, day hospitals, respite care and Meals on Wheels. When living in your own home is no longer possible, sheltered housing is the next best thing. This has communal dining and recreation if needed, but the privacy of your own living accommodation. There are qualified nurses and carers available when help is needed. The problem at present is that sheltered housing is not available in every area in Ireland. When continual care becomes necessary, the options will depend on the circumstances of the individual client. In some areas there are district and community hospitals available. There are also many types of residential care. It is important to explore what options are available in the area. It is also necessary to check the financial aspects and explore the rules and regulations regarding subvention, etc.

Legislation is being developed to provide clear statutory provisions for entitlement to health and social services. Case officers to combat the abuse of older people have been appointed. The government is committed to creating an ombudsman for older people. There are various home-care packages to improve community support. As well as statutory and government services, there are also many voluntary agencies: St Vincent de Paul, Alzheimer's Society of Ireland, The Irish Hospice Foundation and many more. The 'Older and Bolder' campaign is a coalition of five organisations working to improve services for the older person: Age Action Ireland, Age & Opportunity, Irish Senior Citizens Parliament, Irish Hospice Foundation and Senior Help Line. Their aim is to achieve a commitment from the government to develop a national strategy on ageing and older people. It also highlights issues to do with health, employment, transport and income. The introduction of rural transport has improved the lives of older people living in rural areas. A new nursing home care support scheme, 'A Fair Deal', is currently being reviewed by the Department of Health and Children. This new scheme aims to ensure that care will be affordable for all. The new scheme will ensure that care is affordable for all. It is always advisable to check in the community where you live as there are many other individual services available.

'AGE IS HONOURABLE'

The people in your care have lived long and varied but completely individual lives. They deserve to be treated with respect and dignity, and to expect attention to their individual needs, especially those who are unable to speak for themselves.

Assignment Guidelines

FETAC LEVEL 5 CARE FOR THE OLDER PERSON MODULE: D20180

For readers undertaking the above module, either as a stand-alone module or as part of their overall award, this chapter has been written with you in mind. The other chapters in this book are also relevant to the care of the older person. There are two assignments required to complete the module:

Skills Demonstration: 60%

Learners are required to have completed a practical activity in the workplace during which the following skills will be assessed:

- Organisation and preparation of the activity, paying particular attention to meeting the needs of the client
- Ability to carry out the task/activity
- Communications skills
- Adherence to health and safety practices.

A written account of the activity must also be submitted. Examples of activities that may be chosen are:

- Reminiscence therapy session
- An outing to the shops for a wheelchair-bound client
- Music evening, card games, etc.

Project Weighting: 40%

Projects will be based on a brief provided by the internal assessor. The brief will include guidelines for the learner. The learner will choose a topic associated with the care of the older person and in line with the brief. You will need to research/investigate the chosen topic. Identify the needs of the client and discuss the role of the HCA in meeting these needs. You are expected to provide a comprehensive analysis of your findings and recommendations. Reflect on what you have learned and how it will assist you in the care of the older person with a specific condition. Examples of topics include caring for clients with the following conditions: arthritis, incontinence, dementia, Alzheimer's disease or stroke, or any suitable condition/situation of the learner's choice. Your course tutor will normally provide you with detailed briefs for both assignments which will assist you to complete the work.

CHAPTER EIGHT

CHALLENGING BEHAVIOUR MANAGEMENT

Martha McGinn

What is Challenging Behaviour?; Causes of Challenging Behaviour; Risk Assessment and Risk Management; The Role of Staff in Reducing the Risk of Violence and Aggression; Creating Safer Environments; Communication; Identifying Challenging Behaviour at an Early Stage; The Legal and Professional Considerations Required in the Use of Physical Intervention

Introduction

Staff members working in caring services are involved more and more with complex service users who can at times exhibit difficult, challenging and possibly violent behaviour. There is a greater expectation that services respond to these situations in a balanced, professional manner given the publication of the *National Quality Standards for Residential Care Settings for Older People in Ireland* (HIQA, 2008), which states: 'All staff have up-to-date knowledge and skills appropriate to their role, to enable them to manage and respond to behaviour that is challenging (Standard 21, Criteria 21.4, HIQA, 2008). Failure to comply with these standards can result in penalties and/or closure. This chapter is specifically designed for care staff working within a range of care settings to teach them to use appropriate evidence-based responses to service users who may present with difficult behaviour, while providing best care that is legally compliant.

What is Challenging Behaviour?

According to the British Institute of Learning Disabilities (BILD), the term 'challenging behaviour' has come into common usage relatively recently, replacing more traditional descriptions, such as 'problem', 'disruptive' and 'maladaptive'. This shift in terminology signals a move away from a more rigid concentration on the behaviour as a 'problem' intrinsic to the person, towards a greater awareness of the need to examine and understand other aspects of the person's life, the environment in which they live, interactional factors, the impact of their physical and mental wellbeing, as well as personal dimensions. The 'challenge' to us is the systems we have created and the services we provide, and it is our responsibility to respond to this challenge.

Challenging behaviour types include:

- Aggression, particularly in relation to resisting care (such as hitting, kicking, biting, hair-pulling, grabbing hands and clothing, etc)
- Verbal aggression
- Threatening and intimidating behaviour
- Wandering.

Typically, behaviour which is challenging puts the personal safety of the service user and others at risk. It also has a considerable impact on the lives of those who engage in challenging behaviour and perhaps, just as significantly, it can reduce the quality of life of those who are affected.

There are three competencies that members of care staff are required to have in order to be able to keep their service users and themselves safe:

1 Appreciate and develop an awareness of why a service user's behaviour is challenging.
2 Be able to carry out successful risk assessments on service users whose behaviour may challenge.
3 Be able to demonstrate the appropriate responses in particular scenarios ensuring personal safety as well as the safety of others.

Having an appreciation and an awareness of why a service user's behaviour is at times challenging is a complex matter. Failing to develop that appreciation may mean you have little or nothing to offer a person whose behaviour is challenging. Give some thought to when you yourself may get angry: who is the person most likely to calm you down? Is it someone you know well and who understands and appreciates where you are coming from?

Understanding the purpose that challenging behaviour serves for an individual is very important; otherwise we can demonise a service user. If you have no explanation for how someone behaves, you will have only incorrect solutions or no solutions at all. This will result in the service user feeling lonely and isolated and may compound his/her need to be aggressive. The more we understand about a person's behaviour the more we will be able to tolerate their behaviour, which will enable us to cope emotionally and psychologically.

Causes of Challenging Behaviour

There are many factors which determine a service user's behaviour in any given situation, such as:

- Service-user factors
- Staff factors
- Interactional factors
- Environmental factors
- Physiological factors
- Social factors
- Psychological/Cognitive factors
- Mental health factors
- Bereavement, loss and separation
- Treatment-related factors

SERVICE-USER FACTORS

Service users bring their own personal factors to any situation, such as their perspective, their feelings, their unresolved issues, their ability to understand and comprehend the setting in which they find themselves. Their ability to interact and communicate their needs, fears and anxieties and their limitations may impact on their sense of powerlessness and lack of independence. The person's constitution also plays a significant role. This refers to the person's physical state; e.g. allergies, chronic illnesses, sensory impairments, any mental health problem the person is experiencing, plus any drugs they are taking which may affect their behaviour.

It may also be important to consider the impact of any syndrome or disorder, such as autistic spectrum disorder, or condition such as dementia, that the person may have and its effect on behaviour. The person being an extrovert or introvert, moody or impulsive, easily aroused and frustrated, or quiet and passive, will contribute to their behaviour. Poor self-esteem is a direct cause of challenging behaviour. Behaviour will always be compounded by the person's ability to communicate his thoughts, needs and feelings, either verbally or non-verbally. The person's recent past experiences can be a major factor in determining a person's behaviour, such as any changes, loss or bereavement or having been the victim of abuse (sexual or physical).

STAFF FACTORS

Relationships between staff and service users have the potential to add considerably to the quality of a person's life. Service users will look to staff for support and guidance.

Equally staff members bring their personal factors to a situation. Without training, a staff member will bring their perspective, their feelings, their unresolved issues, their ability to understand and comprehend the scenario, their ability to interact and communicate their needs, their fears and anxieties and their limitations. This may impact on the service user's sense of powerlessness and lack of independence. Staff members require training to be able to contain and support a person whose behaviour is challenging.

Poor communication between staff teams can lead to poor organisation, inconsistent care and irritations between staff, which can result in service users' care needs and person-centred needs not been adequately addressed. Inadequate staffing levels can lead to service users being rushed, resulting in dissatisfaction and frustration, which may cause aggressive responses from them.

INTERACTIONAL FACTORS

Various studies have been undertaken with staff to determine the factors that have led to service users being aggressive. Spokes *et al.* (2002) 'found that the majority of the interviewed staff had weaknesses in dealing with patient violence. Actions leading or contributing to an incident mentioned by the nurses in this study were goal prevention, being confrontational, giving medication and being rude or making personal comments.' 'In the study by Finnema this was specified by reporting the fact that the staff behaved inadequately: they did not listen to patients; they failed to keep appointments; they deliberately provoked, neglected and interrupted patients; and they did not understand patients and asked too much of them' (Finnema *et al.*, 1994).

ENVIRONMENTAL FACTORS

Lack of personal space and privacy can cause frustration, as can constant interruptions from others, unpredictable movement and incompatible groups of service users. Irritations between service users is extremely common; research tells us that 70 per cent of service users are subjected to taunts, jibes and insults from their peers. Some service users become challenging if they are subjected to abuse, intimidation, bullying or harassment. It is the role of the staff to protect service users and ensure they are safe and free from abuse. Overcrowded living environments, inadequate lighting, poor ventilation, uncomfortable surroundings with little opportunity for development can all cause a lack of stimulation which in turn can cause frustrations leading to aggressive reactions and overreactions. A lack of freedom on closed units can impose rigid routines and restrict or limit freedom and choice; this can also cause service users to exhibit challenging behaviour.

PHYSIOLOGICAL FACTORS

There are many systems in the body, and each system has a distinct function, but when the system fails, often the only outward sign is the person's behaviour. It is important, therefore, to note changes in the person's behaviour and give consideration to the many physiological factors which might be the cause. According to research, pain often manifests itself in fear and aggression, which staff members do not always recognise. For example, dental pain is often undetected, and, in older persons, arthritic pain is often untreated, while fractures are not always observed if the person has had a fall and is unable to tell someone. Many conditions can cause the person to become aggressive, such as:

- Cerebral vascular accident (stroke), which can cause speech, hearing, mobility and visual impairment, thus causing frustration, anger and agitation
- Type 2 diabetes
- Thyroid dysfunction
- Heart diseases
- Urinary tract infection (UTI)
- Bladder infections
- Renal or kidney dysfunction
- Constipation
- Dehydration and poor nutrition
- Incontinence can cause infection if hygiene is not maintained; this is known as ascending infection
- Any illness which causes an increase in temperature can lead to agitation, such as common colds, bronchitis or pneumonia.

Social factors

Human warmth and kindness is an emotional and social need and therefore intellectual inability does not exclude this need. People in care settings with poor communication skills can become extremely isolated. A smile, a nod, a hand hold or simply sitting with the person are some of the ways that these needs could be met. People need to feel a sense of belonging and to have meaningful relationships. Older people and people with disabilities living in care homes must also cope with the departure of care staff on a regular basis, due to a high turnover in the sector. Isolation and loneliness may cause a person to engage in challenging behaviour as a means of making contact or making a connection with staff.

Psychological/Cognitive factors

'We can no longer assert that when cognitive functioning fails us, all that is left is our physical self. We must attend to the psychological needs of people if we want to improve their wellbeing' (Stokes, 2001). However, privacy and dignity when tending to personal care can sometimes be ignored if staff members feel the person cannot complain. Block treatment, where everyone is treated the same, can result in a person feeling as if they have been denied their individuality, and changes in schedule or rushing a person can cause extreme disappointment, frustration, or fear.

Being treated as an individual and involved in their care are important aspects of dignity for all people. The Health Commission (2007) conducted a survey to identify how services are addressing the need to treat people in care with dignity and found older people did not always feel adequately involved in their own care. Only 55 per cent of older people surveyed said that they felt involved in their care as much as they wanted, while 94 per cent were never asked for their views while they were in long-stay hospital. According to the Alzheimer's Association, 'Poor care does cause the person to feel frustrated and is a common trigger of behaviour which is challenging.'

Other significant factors which will influence a person's behaviour are:
• Unfamiliar environment and not having familiar faces around
• Fear and embarrassment of intimate parts of their body being exposed
• Noisy night-time environment
• Not knowing where to get comfort from
• Being provided with intimate care by many different staff who do not even introduce themselves.

It is important to note that most incidents of aggression occur when providing intimate care. Resistance or aggression may result from a poor approach. It is worth examining your own approach when tending to a person's intimate care needs.

MENTAL HEALTH FACTORS

The majority of older people in care homes, according to a UK survey conducted by Age Concern (2007), have mental health problems, so the provision of high-quality mental healthcare in this setting is vital. Between 50 and 80 per cent of residents have dementia, 40 per cent have depression and high percentages have both. Care-home residents include older people with long-term mental health problems such as schizophrenia who 'graduated' from long-stay hospitals when they closed.

In a study conducted by Prasher (2003) that assessed 207 adults with intellectual disability, 49.2 per cent were found to have a psychiatric disorder and adults with a more severe intellectual disability had higher rates of additional psychiatric disorders. While this study is small, they were randomly selected.

Taylor and Navaco (2005) found that people with intellectual disabilities were particularly vulnerable to mental health difficulties. The reasons they cite are:
• Their environmental settings are 'intrinsically constraining and limited in satisfaction'

- Recurrent frustration of their 'physical, emotional and interpersonal needs not being met can activate anger'
- 'Defective cognitive functioning hinders their coping abilities with aversive events'
- Deprived support systems prevent and diminish their problem-solving options.

Despite these high statistics, many mental health conditions go undetected, undiagnosed and, more significantly, untreated. People can be extremely anxious, agitated and aggressive under these circumstances. According to Age Concern (2007), 'Care-home staff are often undertrained, overwhelmed and generally not well supported to identify and respond to the mental health needs of older people. Staff education and training can lead to increased rates of detection of depression, better treatment and outcomes for older people in care.'

BEREAVEMENT, LOSS AND SEPARATION

People in care have often had more than their fair share of loss and separation. Death of a loved one or deterioration in health can often be the reason for transition into a care home, and this move is often made without the full emotional impact for the person being fully understood by staff. Moving into a care home can be a major life transition that involves considerable loss and, consequently, depression is common among people who have recently moved into a care home.

Older people living in care homes must routinely cope with fellow residents passing away, and may also suffer from the loss of visits from their families. Age Concern (2007) also states that 'older people living in care homes must also cope with the departure of care-home staff on a regular basis, due to high turnover in the sector.'

TREATMENT-RELATED FACTORS

Treatment-related factors can sometimes put us in close contact with service users when they are either already very distressed or they are distressed by the treatment being provided. These factors include:
- Providing intimate care
- Giving medication
- Approaching service users when they are agitated
- Approaching service users who are at risk or engaging in risk-related activities
- Assisting when blood is being taken
- Assisting the person with dental care
- Assisting the person to eat or drink
- Sometimes changes of medication may cause effects which they were not intended to do, such as agitation and wandering.

Risk Assessment and Risk Management

DEFINITIONS

Risk assessment is defined as 'the systematic collection of information to determine the degree to which harm (to self or others) is likely at some point in time' (O'Rourke *et al.*, 2001).

Risk management is the creation of a written plan of action, based on the assessment, to reduce the likelihood of harm actually occurring, balanced against the principles of client/carer choice, safety, normal living and independence.

The following are the most common areas of risk which, as carers, we need to be concerned about:

- Risk to others, which includes physical and psychological risk
- Risk to self, which includes physical and psychological risk
- Care needs being neglected
- Poor quality interaction from staff
- Poor quality-of-life outcomes
- Vulnerability and exploitation

If there is a possibility that any of these areas of risk are anticipated in the healthcare setting, it should be acknowledged as a key health and safety issue, and measures should be put in place to advert it. Minimising the impact of these risks needs to be seen as a priority, and identifying the factors likely to increase the risk and those likely to decrease the risk is often the first step. It is also important to know who is at significant risk, and what factors make them more vulnerable. Behaviours that put people at risk have been dealt with at the beginning of this chapter. The service user, staff and other services that live or work with the person being aggressive are all people who will be exposed to risks and consequences of violence and aggression. The main risks are dealt with in this chapter but they are not exhaustive. The combination of service-user issues, untrained staff and impoverished environment may mean there is little containment in a situation and it could easily escalate out of control.

RISKS TO OTHERS

In a study among nurses on general hospital wards, more than 50 per cent of nurses felt they had become acclimatised to aggression and accepted it as part of the work (Zernike & Sharpe, 1998). In the same study, staff reported that they felt threatened as a result of an incident on 85 per cent of occasions. In the studies on psychiatric wards, about 80 per cent of staff said they felt safe most of the time from physical assault. This could have been due to the fact that they were trained to deal with it. Farrell (1999) found that 30 per cent of the nurses reported that they had experienced aggression almost on a daily basis. Wittington (1996) claimed that A&E departments, learning disability and psychiatric services are traditionally associated with an increased risk of violence.

Risks associated with dealing with aggressive incidents for staff are as follows:

- Stress, anxiety, fear, helplessness, irritation and depression result from staff having to deal with persistent verbal abuse.
- Stress-related health problems, leading to the need for sick leave.
- Psychological problems, as employees may sometimes feel partly to blame for aggressive incidents and, as Marais-Stein (1998) argues, the victims often feel shame and guilt, tend to blame themselves and replay incidents repeatedly in their minds. In severe cases post-traumatic stress may occur.
- Low morale and loss of confidence, affecting their ability to do their job.
- Low productivity resulting from high levels of sick leave, staff refusal to do certain jobs or work with certain service users.
- High levels of violence can also lead to the breakdown in client–professional relationship.

These are very significant risks for staff and need to be factored into the risk assessment.

RISKS TO SELF

People who present with behaviour that is challenging often encounter the following consequences:

- Self-injury
- Containment: reduction in choices and options
- Punishment: reduction in access to services
- Reduction in access to community facilities
- Poor self-esteem
- Reduction in range of activities because of staffing requirements
- Exclusion from services
- Isolation from peers and family
- Staff reluctance to work with people with challenging behaviours.

A vicious cycle may arise as a result of service users' behaviour being a direct result of the consequences imposed for original behaviour.

CARE NEEDS BEING NEGLECTED

A lack of human resources such as psychologists, psychiatrists, social workers, behaviour nurse specialists and occupational therapists can result in a poor or inadequate assessment of service users' needs. This can also lead to the serious risk of undiagnosed and untreated emotional issues, behaviour maladjustment, physical illness and mental illness. Statistics in relation to service users having superimposed mental illness in care varies, but some experts say at least 50 per cent to 70 per cent will suffer a mental illness during their lifetime, and if the lack of services in these areas continues, most will remain undetected and untreated.

POOR QUALITY INTERACTION FROM STAFF

The controlling style of staff, denial of service users' requests, e.g. the request for a cigarette, not listening to service users, interrupting them, not understanding them, being confrontational, making personal comments, being rude, deliberately provoking service users and failure to keep appointments are all interactional factors which might compound and increase the likelihood of a risk of violence and aggression.

POOR QUALITY-OF-LIFE OUTCOMES

Numerous philosophers have tried to explain what is meant by 'quality of life'. They have undertaken extensive research over long periods of time, writing books and articles, etc. Yet John O'Brien, an American psychologist, has simplified the term 'quality of life' into five interlinking accomplishments, namely:

1 Choices
2 Respect and dignity
3 Sharing ordinary places
4 Being able to contribute
5 Meaningful relationships

Each accomplishment supports a vital dimension of human experience which common practice limits for people in care services. Service users' quality of live is often impoverished because, as care services, we often focus solely on a person's disability and trying to manage disabilities by helping or fixing people, instead of appreciating people as people, allowing and supporting them to live their lives as they wish. We also take charge and take over people's lives, instead of allowing freedom of expression and supporting people as they wish to live their lives. This means we do not invest in helping them to pursue meaningful, quality lives where they have status and are seen as valued members of a community. Services pose many restrictions and barriers on their freedom to form meaningful and fulfilling relationships. Services also take control, preventing an individual from having control over their own destiny. All these factors can cause enormous frustration and loss, and life can feel like an existence rather than an opportunity.

There is a very serious risk that service users whose behaviour is challenging, difficult, dangerous and disruptive often have their lives, freedom and choices restricted. This can happen in a variety of ways, such as:

- Access to services may be reduced
- Access to community services may be reduced for fear that members of the public could get injured
- Additional staff are put in place to provide a safe environment, which leads to a policing of movement
- Exclusion from mainstream services
- Staff may be fearful of service user and may not want to take chances so they restrict their outings.

Vulnerability and Exploitation

According to Trust in Care Policy (2005) 'the term "abuse" can be subject to wide interpretation. Abuse is considered to be any form of behaviour that violates the dignity of patients/clients. Abuse may consist of a single act or repeated acts. It may be physical, sexual, financial or psychological and emotional. It may constitute neglect and poor professional practice. Some statistics suggest that people with challenging behaviour in care are most vulnerable to abuse, and often by their carers. Challenging behaviour may be the only outward sign that abuse is occurring in a person's life.

The Role of Staff in Reducing the Risk of Violence and Aggression

The primary directive of a nurse in relation to the management of violence is always towards its prevention. Only if preventative measures have failed will the carer's role be directed towards maintaining the safety and wellbeing of the service user and those involved in the incident (An Bord Altranais guidance on the management of violence/challenging behaviour, 1997).

While this book is for HCAs, it is a good guide for all staff working in the caring services. Good observations of changes in the person's behaviour may lead to determining if the person is in pain or unwell, and may prevent the person becoming aggressive. Remember aggression is always a sign that something is wrong. Think about your interaction with the person, step back and give the person space.

It is vitally important that staff act to de-escalate a service user's behaviour and call for assistance in the event of a service user being aggressive. Staff members need to take reasonable care for their own safety at work and the safety of those affected by their actions; this includes service users and colleagues. More and more services have a policy on managing violence and aggression and it is important that the actions of staff are consistent with the policy guidelines:

- Ensure all incidents of violence are recorded and reported prior to going off duty
- Inform manager of any hazards which exist
- Avoid situations where there is a known risk of violence
- Follow local procedures for safe working practices
- Seek advice from senior staff if you are unsure of any situation.

Creating Safer Environments

Safer environments can be created by all staff participating in the development of person-centred plans, care plans, risk assessments and action plans for each service user so that preventative measures can be devised. Increasing the quality of a person's life experience should be an important goal for the staff team, rather than merely managing a person's behaviour. Adopting a facilitative and enabling approach rather than a controlling style will also help to create a safer environment. Creating a friendly, warm environment is by far the most preventative measure.

- Get to know service users well and develop a good rapport with them.
- Encourage service users to confide in you if they appear upset.
- Participate actively in handovers and meetings and communicate all relevant information and observations with regard to service users.
- Keep appointments.
- Ensure good working relationships with colleagues.
- Take part in assessment of service users.
- Ensure service users are treated fairly at all times.
- Ensure service users' complaints are dealt with quickly and fairly.

Communication

Very often the only control the carer has in situations is their own behaviour. Being able to recognise the personal factors which may influence a person's behaviour will usually mean you can develop empathy and make a connection with the person, especially if you can communicate your understanding to the person (*see* Chapter 5). This will give you a good understanding of how to communicate with a service user when they are feeling angry. It is important to realise that being angry is a natural and healthy feeling. There are numerous advantages to being angry: society may never have developed if no one got frustrated and angry about not being able to communicate. That anger drove the development of the telephone! Getting angry may also spur us on to telling someone how we feel; this can result in beneficial changes to how things get done. However, these are healthy responses to anger. What makes someone go from being angry to being physically aggressive is the subject of much research. One piece of research asked service users why they got violent and they said it was because staff members were upholding agency rules, preventing them from doing something and/or giving direct instructions.

This means that staff members using an authoritative and directive style are more at risk of being injured or hurt than staff members using a facilitative style that does not attempt to overpower the service user.

Identifying Challenging Behaviour at an Early Stage

Aggression is the end point of someone's distress and anger. Service users, like everyone, will go through four stages prior to getting aggressive:

1   Anxiety stage
2   Verbal aggression stage
3   Physical aggression stage
4   Recuperation phase.

1. ANXIETY STAGE

There is an obvious increase or change in behaviour in person's energy, such as:

- Pacing
- Tapping
- Agitation
- Biting nails
- Crying
- Becoming withdrawn.

Interventions at this stage need to include:

- Try to convey the sense that the situation needs to be sorted out *together*. Using the word 'we' can be helpful in communicating this
- Active listening, empathic approach. Let them know you care they are upset
- Keep asking questions in order to convey your desire to see the situation from their point of view. However, avoid asking why the person became upset as retelling can increase arousal
- Reflect back on what the person is telling you; for instance say 'so you feel misunderstood', in order to reassure them that you are taking in what they are saying
- Give your undivided attention; suggest they sit down and tell you everything that is worrying them.

* Don't trivialise

2. VERBAL AGGRESSION STAGE

Service user will start:
* Shouting, being verbally abusive
* Personalise issues
* Uses threats and verbal intimidation
* Vent at anyone and anything.

Interventions will need to be:
* Acknowledgement of their frustration and anger
* Stick to the issue, don't wander off it, and bring service users back to the issue if they try to wander off
* Isolate situation; remove others from the situation to ensure they remain safe and to avoid an audience effect
* Set limits; don't let them use you as an emotional punchbag
* Follow protocol/guidelines that your organisation or team have adopted
* Allow verbal release, don't interrupt
* Wait for pauses or gaps before you say anything
* Reset limits/protocol/guidelines
* Remove anything you think may be used as a weapon.

Non-verbal behaviour
Try to present a calm reaction to aggression by relaxing your muscles and move slowly:
* Position
* Body buffer zones
* Voice
* Eye contact
* Touch

Position
* Try to stand or sit at an angle of about 45 degrees to the person rather than opposite them. Also, if sitting, ensure that the chairs are of equal height.

Body buffer zones
* Habitually aggressive people often need bigger buffer zones, so keep a greater distance.

Voice

- Speak unhurriedly and softly and in a tone that is neither judgmental nor patronising.

Eye contact

- This heightens emotion; therefore beware of excessive eye contact and avoid it entirely if this appears to reduce the tension.

Touch

- Touch is an ambiguous signal and even sympathetic touch can be perceived as a threat
- The general rule is not to touch the person, but to keep a distance between you
- However, there may be situations where you know the person well, in which case touch may have a calming effect
- The critical issue is the need to be sensitive to the individual's needs and how they will be perceived.

Verbal behaviour

Whether or not restraint needs to be used, listen carefully to what the person is saying and try to convey a respect for them and a willingness to try to understand what is disturbing them. Communicate that you want to try to help.

3. PHYSICAL AGGRESSION STAGE

Every effort needs to be made to avoid this stage, but if it does get to this stage the following behaviours will be noticeable:

- Loss of emotional control
- Physical assault
- Use of objects as weapons
- Self-injurious behaviour.

Staff intervention

For this stage the intervention from staff may be to contain the situation as best they can. Remove others from danger, move to a place of safety if you can, providing you have not left the person to obvious risks. The law allows you to use physical skills to protect yourself and defend others when an actual assault is occurring. Where possible, try to assess whether you need to summon help before intervening. Avoid heroics.

Physical restraint should only be used as a last resort, and only if serious harm would be anticipated if such action were not taken. If physical contact cannot be avoided, use only the minimum force necessary to extricate yourself from an attack or to control the situation. However, there is a complex maze of legalities that have to be considered and it is advisable to train in the professional management of aggression and violence.

4. RECUPERATION STAGE

This stage is just as significant as all the others. There is a real danger that if this stage is not handled appropriately the service user could go through this cycle again. Therefore it is important to:

- Assist the service user to regain control
- Allow the service user to be remorseful; don't keep reminding them of what they did, you can have that discussion later
- The service user may be frightened and afraid of punishment or retaliation. They will need your reassurance
- The service user will be tired and quiet.

Staff intervention

- Re-engagement and reassurance are very important
- Positive support/non-verbal behaviour
- Help the service user to develop coping mechanisms and develop strategies so they do not have to get to this level of stress in the future.

The Legal and Professional Considerations Required in the Use of Physical Intervention

Placing a hand on another person without their consent could be unlawful. A defence against this is that it was necessary; you set out to do no harm, you were acting in their best interests and it was fair and just. Inaction is not an option if someone is causing harm to themselves or others. However, failure to convince someone that your actions were justified and fair could end up being judged by your employer or in a court of law with serious consequences.

Assignment Guidelines

FETAC LEVEL 5 CHALLENGING BEHAVIOUR MANAGEMENT MODULE

For readers undertaking the above module, either as a stand-alone module or as part of their overall award, this chapter has been written with you in mind. There are two assignments required to complete the module.

Project weighting: 60%

Learners will be required to demonstrate their understanding of service users who have challenging behaviour and their specific needs. You will need to investigate the chosen topic area and identify how it affects the service user and their family. Identify the treatments available to relieve symptoms experienced by the service user. Discuss the effect this situation has on the client and their family and the role of the healthcare staff. Identify the communication and interpersonal skills required to deal sensitively and appropriately with the client and their family.

Skills demonstration weighting: 40%

This assignment gives the learner an opportunity to focus on three practical skills in dealing with behaviour that is challenging in a controlled environment. Your course provider will normally devise detailed briefs for both assignments which will assist you to complete the work.

CHAPTER NINE

PALLIATIVE CARE SUPPORT
Blathnaid Connolly

History and Definition of Palliative Care; How is Palliative Care Practised?; Where is Palliative Care Practised?; Palliative Care Team; Coping Skills for Patients and Family; The Role of the Healthcare Assistant; Communication Skills in Palliative Care; Management of Symptoms; Terminal Care; Last Offices; Cultural Considerations; Bereavement; Palliative Care for Children

Introduction

You matter because you are you, and you matter to the last moment of your life. We will do all we can to help you, not only to die peacefully but to live until you die.

Dame Cecily Saunders

Some people who choose to enter the caring profession have experienced death and dying from personal experience. Others may have no experience of it, and can be frightened by the idea that they may witness the death of a patient or client and won't know what to do. Death is not often a subject openly talked about and is still considered by some to be taboo. However, in Ireland many people feel that they would like to discuss death and dying, particularly with regard to where they would like to die and what aspects of their care are important to them (Irish Hospice Foundation, 2004). Although most people when asked state they would prefer to die at home, surrounded by people they love, the majority of people actually die in hospital or in an institution (NACPC, 2001).

As people age they realise that dying at home may not be possible for many reasons; there may not be support available, they may feel they would be an unnecessary burden to their family and would not feel comfortable with relatives providing personal care; or they do not wish to have professionals coming into their home (Gott *et al.* 2004). Some of those who have experienced a death of their relative in an Irish hospital feel there is room for improvement in the care provided (Irish Hospice Foundation, 2004). Issues such as poor communication and staff being too busy to provide adequate care, or focusing too much on physical care and not on the psychological or social needs of their patient have been highlighted as areas that need addressing (NACPC, 2001). Participants in a 1999 debate on the principles of a good death felt that there was a variety of factors which they viewed as important about death and dying, such as having knowledge and information about their illness and getting the required expertise when needed, and wanting to retain control over their life and death. Being able to share the experience with those important to them and having time to say goodbye, but not prolonging life unnecessarily, was also considered significant (cited *End of Life Care*, 1:1 2007).

The challenge for those in a caring role is to ensure that all people, regardless of where they die, are afforded the same right to dignity and privacy and to ensure that they and their family receive high-quality care.

This chapter introduces the reader to palliative care. This is a relatively modern concept which focuses on the specific needs of an individual and their family when an illness or disease has no cure. Your role as a healthcare assistant in palliative care will be discussed. The skills and qualities necessary to be able to care for your patient and their family at this difficult time are highlighted. Effective communication is the cornerstone of palliative care; it is essential to learn the different styles of communication and the appropriate time to use them. When a person is terminally ill they will have physical symptoms such as pain and fatigue in addition to complications caused by their medical history. As a healthcare assistant it is important to understand these signs and symptoms so that you can assist the nurse in managing them. However, the psychological impact of living with imminent death is often the biggest burden that patients and their families carry. Kubler-Ross (1970) identified the different coping mechanisms patients have to be able to live each day with their illness. To practise palliative care it is important to understand what these are, so that you are able to provide care that meets your patient's needs and those of their family, not the healthcare practitioner's perception of what their patient needs.

Caring for someone in the last days of their life is of paramount importance as memories of how a loved one is cared for will be carried by relatives and friends for many years after their death. If their experience is a positive one this can help them to grieve properly. If they have negative feelings about the quality of care received, this can profoundly affect their future experiences, not just of death and dying but also of the healthcare service as a whole. At the end of life patients will often display certain physical symptoms and are very dependent on healthcare staff. Their family are also often very distressed. Certain practices and protocols must be followed in addition to providing high-quality care, often in circumstances that are not ideal. The role of the healthcare assistant is vital, especially in supporting the nursing staff, both during this time and after the patient has died.

History and Definition of Palliative Care

The World Health Organisation has defined palliative care as: 'An approach that improves the quality of life of patients and their families facing the problems associated with life-threatening illness, through the prevention and relief of suffering by means of early identification and impeccable assessment and treatment of pain and other problems, physical, psychosocial and spiritual' (World Health Organisation, 1990).

We are living longer because of advances in medical technology and our increasing knowledge of how to prevent and manage disease. By the 1950s most people were dying in hospitals instead of at home, and death was seen as failure because a cure was not found. Consequently people often died not only in severe pain, but coping with their suffering and that of their families with little support and understanding. Although hospices had been in existence for many centuries, they originally provided much-needed care for the sick poor, and in some cases were called homes for incurables. Palliative care differs from terminal care, as it can begin very early on in diagnosis. Terminal care is a continuation of palliative care because it is concerned with the last days or weeks of life. Dame Cecily Saunders, founder of St Christopher's Hospice in London in 1967, is considered the pioneer of the palliative care movement as we know it now. Firstly as a nurse and social worker, then as a doctor, she witnessed what she defined as the 'total pain' of the dying patient. Her aim was to alleviate suffering by providing true holistic care; where physical symptoms of disease and the psychological, social and emotional impact of impending loss for the patient and family are managed in equal measure. This changed the way the healthcare profession viewed death and dying. The hospice foundation was founded in 1986 to support the development of palliative care in Ireland.

How is Palliative Care Practised?

When a person is told that they require palliative care this does not mean that treatment is no longer available. The focus of care switches to treating the symptoms of the illness or disease, but no cure is expected. Some people will have been ill for some time; often they may have undergone rigorous treatments including surgery, various drug therapies and prolonged hospital stays. For people with cancer, radiotherapy and chemotherapy can be involved. For others the chronic disease which they have lived with for many years may have progressed to the extent that palliative care is now appropriate. Whatever the circumstances the news that someone has a life-threatening illness is devastating for them and their loved ones. Palliative care does not aim to provide a cure; rather it accepts that dying is part of a normal process and the quality of the patient's life must be maintained for as long as they are alive. For many they can be receiving this type of care for weeks, months or even years. Palliative care can be complex in its management; the aim of treatment is to alleviate the suffering felt by the patient. In fact, many people continue with intensive treatment to control the side effects of their illness.

Key principles of the palliative care approach include:

1. Focus on quality of life.
2. Good symptom control.
3. A holistic approach that takes into account the person's life experience and current situation.
4. Care that encompasses both the dying person and those that matter to that person.
5. Emphasis on open and sensitive communication across the care providers, patients and family (National Advisory Committee on Palliative Care, 2001).

Where is Palliative Care Practised?

Most, if not all, large acute hospitals have a palliative care team. They will receive referrals from other medical teams and manage patients requiring palliative care in the hospital setting. Patients remain in their own wards and the palliative care team work closely with other doctors and nurses. In addition to this they will also refer patients to other services in the community, especially in preparation for discharge to a home if and when appropriate. The general practitioner (GP) and the public heath nurse (PHN) are responsible for caring for patients in the community, whether in their own home, nursing home or other community facility. Many community hospitals will have designated palliative care beds which can be accessed by the GP. Patients may be admitted there for management of their symptoms, for respite to allow rest for them and their carers, and often for care at the end of life. There are also specialist palliative care units, known in some areas as hospices. Often people think that when a person is referred to the hospice they will die soon. However these units provide many services. It is the base for the home-care team, specialists working in the community providing advice and support to patients, families and the GP and PHN. Patients can also attend the day centre, which offers many services to support those living at home. There are also in-patient beds where patients can be admitted for management of their symptoms, respite care or for end-of-life care. Much needed bereavement support is provided to the patients' loved ones during their illness and after death. Currently in Ireland there are eight such specialist units.

Palliative Care Team

Some of the services provided by specialist palliative care units can be seen in Figure 9.1 below:

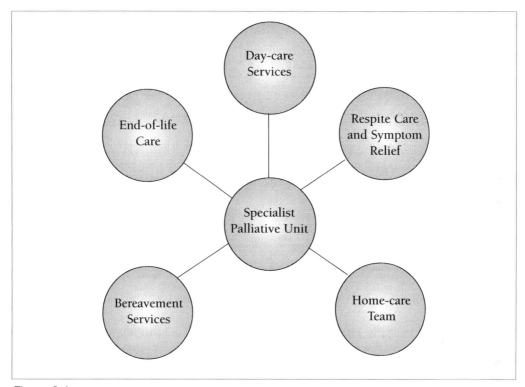

Figure 9.1

Each specialist palliative care unit contains a team of people with a variety of skills and knowledge. Figure 9.2 (on page 138) outlines some of the people who may be in the palliative care team.

The voluntary services contribute significantly to palliative care provision in Ireland. In addition to essential fundraising, they provide support during the day and night. This can relieve the pressure often felt by carers who wish to keep their dying relative at home, but can become tired and need a break.

Currently in Ireland 95 per cent of people availing of the palliative care service have cancer (Irish Hospice Foundation, 2005), but there has been a recent increase in non-cancer patients requiring palliative care. People with Motor Neurone Disease (MND), Acquired Immune Deficiency Syndrome (AIDS), Multiple Sclerosis (MS) and some progressive chronic diseases, also benefit from palliative care. This means there is an increasing demand for palliative care, not just in Ireland but globally, as people are facing

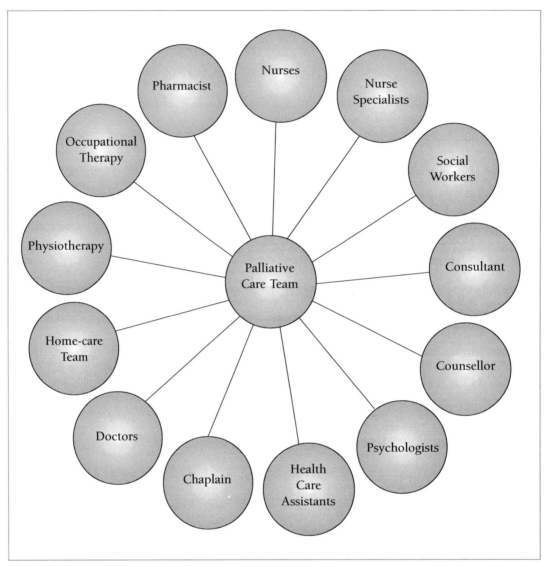

Figure 9.2

many challenges related to life-threatening illness and need expert care. There is limited information available on the delivery of palliative care services in Ireland. It appears that services differ depending on where you live; in some areas there are no specialist in-patient units and limited home-care services (Irish Hospice Foundation, 2005). The National Advisory Committee on Palliative Care (NACPC), which was established by the Department of Health and Children, reported in 2001. They have made many recommendations on how palliative care can and should be developed in Ireland. One of the most significant of these is that palliative care should be offered in all areas of care when appropriate. This may involve understanding the general principles of palliative care, or more in-depth training of staff on how to deliver palliative care in their setting. In addition to this, an expansion of the specialist service is required to meet the needs of the growing population.

What type of knowledge and skills do you think would be needed to practice palliative care where you work?

Coping Skills for Patients and Family

Imagine what it must be like to be told that you are very ill and there is no cure, or that the treatment you are having for your illness is not working. How would you cope? What would your first thoughts be?

Dr Elizabeth Kubler-Ross, a psychiatrist working in America in the 1970s, wrote a book called *On Death and Dying*. This book is a collection of conversations she and her team had with patients who were terminally ill, and in some cases their families. She identified through her work that people experience different emotions, often called the stages of grief. They are, in fact, normal feelings that a person will go through at different times from when they are first diagnosed up until death. It is not just the patient, but their loved ones and sometimes the healthcare staff who experience these feelings. Although they are explained in different stages, this does not mean the person feels them in succession; they can move back and forth through the different stages.

STAGES OF GRIEF

Stage One: Denial

'This can't be true': a very normal reaction to bad news, we do it all the time when we experience loss, large or small. For your patients, they need this; it acts as a defence mechanism and allows them time to gather their thoughts and for the information to sink in. Sometimes your patient will not discuss it, and may even change the subject.

What is the role of the care worker? You need to listen to and observe your patient. Follow their lead; don't push or persuade the person to talk. They need time and space to deal with the shock. This stage normally lasts only a short time.

Stage Two: Anger

Often this follows denial. The person can be angry for many reasons and direct it in different ways. They can feel anger towards doctors and nurses because their treatment didn't work, or at themselves because they feel they should have taken better care of their health, or even at life itself, because theirs is being cut short. Anger can come out in different ways; some of us shout and scream, some people become silent and withdrawn, and often people say hurtful things. As a healthcare worker it can be very hard to deal with a person's anger. It is important not to take it personally; put yourself in the person's place and try to empathise. Ask yourself: why are they like this? How would I feel? It is important to remain calm in the face of another's aggression. Becoming angry yourself is inappropriate, and will only inflame the situation further. Always report your experiences to the nurse in charge; it is important that they know what is happening and they can also support you.

Stage Three: Bargaining

This can be done privately, or often with God. I want to get to Christmas, or be at my child's wedding. How many times have you heard about people making these types of bargains when they are dying? It may not come true, but they need this to sustain themselves. However, they may be feeling guilty about leaving people behind. If a person appears to be bargaining in your presence, do not ignore it; tell the nurse in charge. Again you need to listen and not give false hope. As a healthcare worker it can be tempting to reassure the person by telling them that everything will be alright. In reality you do not know for how long they will live. You need to examine your own feelings about death and dying. Are you saying this to the patient because you are finding their questions or statements difficult to hear? Again this is perfectly normal. Caring for someone who is terminally ill can be very rewarding and tiring at the same time. If you have experienced loss this can affect how you deal with your patients. It can bring up feelings of your own grief. This can be very positive, because you can empathise with your patient and their relatives. However, if you are afraid of death and dying, as many people are, you may find it hard to deal with someone talking about it and brush over their comments by saying things like, 'It will be OK', or ignoring them altogether. This is not constructive or helpful to them.

Ask yourself: how do I feel about dying? What am I afraid of? Reflect on experiences you may have had with patients in the past, and think about the effect they had on you. Was it a positive or negative experience? Why? What could have been done differently? This will help you in your role, and it will have a positive effect on how you care for your patients.

Stage Four: Depression

According to Dr Kubler-Ross, there are two different types of depression experienced by the patient, both associated with the overwhelming feelings of loss. Think of all the things they have lost: their physical health; maybe their ability to move or do things for themselves; they could be supporting their family so they have lost their financial independence; perhaps they have lost their status in society or in their family. And then there is the loss to come, death and its finality, which means losing what is left behind, family, friends, children, pets . . . life. They need to be able to express these feelings of loss. In the healthcare profession we can be very good at looking after the person's physical needs, but often to the detriment of their emotional and psychological needs. As a care assistant, you must report your observations to the nurse, e.g. if your patient seems withdrawn or not eating, or saying that they feel depressed. Medication may be prescribed to help the person cope with it. Depression is normal, but can be difficult to witness; we often like to be able to 'fix what is wrong'. Let your patient know it is OK to feel this way. Non-verbal communication may be more appropriate, just being there for your patient and showing you understand can make a big difference to them as they come to terms with their feelings of grief.

Fifth Stage: Acceptance

Not all people will reach a stage of acceptance; in fact not all people will visit each stage. When the person accepts their fate, they may feel peace; they may also want to sort out their affairs, make plans and say goodbye to people. They may wish to talk openly about their death. Although this is a normal process, it can be very difficult for their loved ones who are not as accepting. The role of healthcare staff is to support the family, not to push them to accept the reality but to talk to them and listen to their fears and anxieties. You may also find it difficult to hear your patient talk so openly about their death. Don't be mistaken in thinking it is a happy time for them, acceptance is just that; it can happen many weeks or months before the actual death, and patients can often go back to another stage of grief after acceptance. Although not called a stage of grief, the one thing that is maintained throughout the person's illness is the feeling of hope. It should never be underestimated how crucial hope is. It keeps people going in times of deep despair. Terminally ill patients have said that the one part of care they find difficult is when communicating with staff their hope appears to be cruelly taken away, mostly because of poor communication skills (NACPC, 2001; Kubler-Ross, 1970). Hope can help the patient to find meaning in their situation.

The Role of the Healthcare Assistant

As a healthcare assistant, what is your role when dealing with patients as they experience the stages of grief? What difficulties do you think you may have caring for patients and families who are going through this?

All members of the healthcare team must understand the stages of grief and must be prepared to listen and spend time with their patients. It is more valuable to sit and listen than spend time trying to avoid the conversation for fear that the patient may get upset.

Kubler-Ross (1970) found that when patients were able to talk about their illness, particularly towards the end of their life, they became less depressed and more communicative; it also helped them to be more accepting of what was to come.

FAMILY

Before discussing the needs of the 'family' or relatives, we need to think about what family is. In palliative care family is defined differently than in other contexts. It really is determined by the patient.

Think of all the people we may consider as our family or loved ones. It is whoever matters to us; the people we want to share our life with. When we are ill our family can be something else: our carers. In palliative care families need a huge amount of support. They are often the main carers in the home and need support, not just emotional support. Time for a break from the caring role can help them to cope and prevent exhaustion and possible breakdown (NACPC, 2001). As visitors the patient's loved ones can feel isolated and confused. Good communication is very important, and being involved as much as possible in the patient's care will allow the family to feel that they can be useful and that they are needed.

Communication Skills in Palliative Care

You have already covered communication in Chapter 5. However let us examine the specific skills we have already mentioned. The ability to listen and empathise with your patient is essential. By listening we do two things: we learn about our patient, their concerns, fears, anxieties and hopes, and we show that we care about what they are saying. In palliative care we can't offer much to someone who is dying, but we can try our best to help them to live. Avoiding patients because you are afraid they may want to talk about death or because you are worrying that they might actually die in your presence is quite common. Remember you don't have to have all the answers, but showing you care will mean much more to your patient. Try to see it from their perspective; they may be feeling isolated and alone. They may not want to talk at all, but enjoy the company. Non-verbal communication such as touch, silence and simply your presence shows your patient that you are there if they need you. Families also appreciate your contact; seeing that their relative is being well cared for will help to alleviate some of their fears and any feelings of guilt they may have. The environment is also very important. It isn't realistic for there to be peace and quiet all the time. A patient who requires palliative care should have their own room. If this isn't possible, they and their family should be allowed privacy and space. As the patient's condition deteriorates they should be allowed visitors more often if they can cope with it. Time is limited and the quality of that time is precious. In specialist palliative care units, visiting is not restricted. In other facilities where people are dying it may be difficult to accommodate this, but special compensation can often be made to respect the dying patient's needs and those of their family.

Management of Symptoms

COMMON SYMPTOMS EXPERIENCED BY PATIENT

Your patient will experience many different symptoms, related to their illness or caused by the treatment of their disease. We will discuss some of the more common ones they may suffer.

Pain

The majority of patients receiving palliative care will experience pain at some point and as their disease progresses it can become more severe. This does not mean, however, that suffering from pain is inevitable and therefore untreatable. Understandably, most people are fearful of experiencing pain. Upon diagnosis of illness or being advised to receive treatment, the first question a person will often ask is: 'will it cause pain?' Such is the extent of that fear. Pain will not only have a physical effect on the patient but, if left untreated, can have damaging psychological effects such as depression, withdrawal, needless suffering and poor quality of life. It is all-consuming for the patient and traumatic to observe for family and caregivers. Pain has been defined as 'an unpleasant emotional and sensory experience' (Watson & Lucas, 2003). This definition does not appear to give weight to the true extent of trauma pain. It can derive from the disease itself or previous chronic disease, be a side effect of treatment, or be the result of factors associated with being ill, such as pressure sores or constipation. Health professionals often underestimate the level of pain experienced by the patient, whilst the family may unknowingly overestimate their relative's pain. Therefore the best and most accurate person to assess the level and extent of pain is the patient themselves (Scottish Intercollegiate Guidelines Network (SIGN), 2000) However, patients, particularly older people, will often under-report the level of pain they experience (Morrison & Meier, 2003). This can be for many reasons; perhaps they feel it is something they must get used to, or their experience of pain management has been poor, so they feel there is nothing that can be done. In reality the majority of pain in palliative care can be controlled, or its severity reduced with appropriate management (SIGN, 2000). Management of pain in palliative care requires a comprehensive approach. The patient must be physically examined by the doctor. In addition to this, the history, location and type of pain, along with the physical effects on mobility, sleep patterns and the effect on the person's mood, are some of the factors which must be assessed by the nurse and doctor. There are a variety of assessment tools and charts used by healthcare staff to provide accurate and documented assistance. The most reliable source is the patient: pain will be better managed if they are involved in their pain assessment and allowed to have some control of their situation (Watson & Lucas, 2003). It is important also to remember that one person's experience of pain differs from another. What may be unbearable pain to one person can have minimal effect on someone else. There are many treatments available to control pain; medication in the form of tablets, liquid injection and patches are common forms of pain relief. Patient-controlled analgesia pumps (PCA) and syringe drivers are also used. The World Health Organisation (WHO) recommends in palliative care that as the person's pain worsens their treatment should intensify. The nurse and doctor will assess and discuss this with the patient and their family, and will often seek advice from the specialist team. It is important to access all treatment available. Effective communication is vital, so patients and family are aware of the side effects of the medication. Other non-medication treatments that are often used include hypnotherapy, acupuncture, massage and complementary therapies. These different treatments can provide relief to the patient. Management of pain continues as the illness progresses and the nurses and doctors should evaluate if the pain control is working. The healthcare assistant's role is vital. During the time you spend with the patient you may observe them in pain or they may tell you that they have pain, but may not have told other people. It is vital that this is reported to the nurse in charge. In addition to this you can provide comfort measures that may help to alleviate their distress, such as a warm bath or a massage.

Nausea and vomiting

Sixty per cent of palliative care patients will experience nausea, whilst 30 per cent will suffer from vomiting (Morrison & Meier, 2003). It can be incapacitating for the patient if they suffer for a prolonged period of time. There can be many causes of nausea and vomiting, so again thorough assessment is required. It can often be treated successfully with medication, but the underlying cause must be found if treatment is to be successful. Your role is to provide comfort for the patient and report to the nurse if they are experiencing nausea or are vomiting. If the person cannot tolerate large amounts of food, they should be provided with what they enjoy in small quantities.

Sore mouth/Dry mouth

Almost all palliative care patients suffer from this. It is extremely common and, if not detected and treated, will get much worse. There are many causes: it could be due to certain medications, mouth breathing or because the patient isn't able to manage their own oral hygiene. It also occurs if the patient is not eating or drinking much because saliva production slows down. A dry mouth can become sore very quickly because of infections such as oral thrush. Often it can go untreated because the patient may not consider it serious enough to mention (Watson & Lucas, 2003). The key to managing this problem is preventing it happening in the first place. If patients are aware that it may happen they will be more likely to report it. Encouraging oral fluids is essential to produce saliva and prevent the mouth from drying out. If your patient cannot tolerate oral fluids, it is essential to provide thorough oral hygiene every two hours. It is also important to keep dentures clean and free from bacteria. The healthcare staff must also remember that patients may not be able to report a sore or dry mouth because they are confused or unconscious.

Other symptoms the patient may experience can be constipation, breathlessness and fatigue. As a healthcare assistant you will spend large portions of the day providing personal care to your patient, so your observation and reporting skills are vital. Even something you may consider minor, like the person saying they don't feel their medication is working, is important to report back to the nurse. Often patients say things as passing comments because they don't realise the significance of it, or they feel nothing can be done, so reporting your concerns can lead to a more comprehensive assessment of the patient's needs.

Terminal Care

You may have heard of someone being told they have six months to live or nurses and doctors may have told you about a patient whose death is imminent. In fact, it is impossible to say when someone will actually die. In palliative care, when a patient is terminally ill, it normally means that their condition is getting progressively worse – over weeks, days or hours. Your patient will require more assistance with the activities of daily living and they may be confined to bed as they are sleeping for longer periods or feel too weak to get up. Intake of food and fluids tends to become less and less. It is important that the family know that this is because their illness is deteriorating and their weakness is not a result of less food. We associate eating and drinking with health and living and relatives sometimes find this hard to accept. The patient will also be unable to take medication orally and alternative routes must be found, normally through a syringe driver or suppositories. Where possible the patient should continue to make decisions regarding their care, as they can become distressed if they feel they are not being kept informed. As they become weaker their family should be involved in decision-making. This is a very anxious time for the patient and family; they may be aware that death is imminent and inevitable, and that is frightening. The family should be allowed and encouraged to participate in caring for their relative; it helps them to feel they are contributing and takes their mind off the situation. In good palliative care, discussions about the patient's wishes in the event of death should have already taken place. It is not appropriate or realistic to have these discussions at this point in time. For nurses and HCAs, their role is to provide high-quality holistic care. You must prevent further illness or injury in the form of pressure sores, mouth problems, constipation or urinary problems. Your aim should be to make the experience as stress free and peaceful as possible; every person has the right to die with dignity and in comfort.

The importance of communicating well with the family cannot be underestimated. They must be kept informed at all times and be allowed to ask questions and feel they have some control over the situation.

In the last three to four days of life there are signs indicating that the person is approaching death. More experienced staff will often be aware that a person may be near death. There tends to be a rapid deterioration in the person's physical health, they become increasingly weak and drowsy or unable to sustain conversation. Their skin will feel cool and clammy to touch. It can appear blotchy or mottled and have a grey pallor. Breathing can be very noisy or moist sounding, caused by fluid in the lungs and airways. Family often find this distressing to listen to; medication can be given for this but it isn't always successful. When awake, the patient can be restless or agitated, again causing distress to the relatives and staff. There may be an underlying cause for this. Factors such as pain, discomfort or constipation must be ruled out by the nursing and medical staff to provide relief to the patient. Even if the patient appears unconscious, they can still hear and understand people around them. Their relatives should be encouraged to talk to them. Also care staff should talk to the patient, let them know they are there. Particularly before carrying out personal care, you should tell the patient what you are going to do. The quality of care should not be compromised because the person is unconscious. It is important to tend to the patient regularly, even when you are busy. Often unconscious, dying patients in side rooms can be forgotten because of other demands placed on staff. Family should be allowed to stay as much as they want at this time, but they should be encouraged to take breaks. Let them know where they can get tea/coffee/sandwiches, etc. as it can be a tiring and very tense time for them. The environment should be calm and quiet; often difficult in a busy ward or unit. When providing care or spending time with the patient, try not to appear rushed. Memories of how a loved one is cared for stay with families for a long time.

LOOK AFTER YOURSELF

Working in care is challenging most of the time. Caring for a dying patient and their family can be rewarding, but stressful, particularly if it is a new experience for you or it is not a common occurrence where you work. The team you work with are very important; you should support each other. Talk about how you feel rather than bottling it up. Try to do this before you finish your shift rather than going home upset. Sharing experiences with other team members will help all of you. Always tell the nurse in charge if you are finding any aspect of the care particularly difficult. It is important that they know this.

AFTER THE PATIENT HAS DIED

Your workplace will have a local protocol or policy on how to provide care to a patient after they have died. The nursing staff will provide guidance on the correct procedures. After the patient passes away, the nurse will inform the doctor who will confirm the death and record the time and date in the medical notes. Paperwork and documentation is very important and is filled out by the nursing and medical staff.

The deceased person's body must be straightened, with one pillow under the head and another beneath the jaw to keep the mouth closed. Gently pressing on the eyelids will close them; tape is not needed but damp gauze may help. A sheet should cover the person's body but not face, and arms can be left out so the family can touch the deceased. The body is then left for an hour before last offices are performed. The nurse will inform the next of kin if they are not present.

Last Offices

Again all areas will follow their own protocol. There are no rules as such to carrying out the last offices. The following practices are commonly carried out:
1. Skin cleaned of bodily fluids; full washing is not always necessary (ideally carried out by two people).
2. Medical equipment is removed by nurse unless the patient is to go to the coroner.
3. Remove all jewellery unless specifically asked not to by the relatives.
4. Wounds are covered with adhesive skin dressings.
5. Orifices are not packed unless there is obvious leakage; use a pad.
6. Dentures should be left in place, or, if this is not possible, put in a labelled denture pot.
7. Property and valuables should be clearly labelled and documented in the property list and given to relatives at an appropriate time.

The nurse documents all notes and appropriate forms. It is acceptable to talk to the patient if this makes you more comfortable. This is the last time you will provide personal care for them; it is important to be respectful and carry out your tasks with dignity and respect for the deceased. Also you must consider other patients in the area; the nurse will talk to them and let them know what is happening as they can also be distressed.

Cultural Considerations

Irish society has over 160 nationalities living here (Census, 2006). This presents challenges in palliative care in different contexts. Firstly people working in care may come from different cultural backgrounds to their patients and are not familiar with their beliefs or value systems. It is important that you do not impose your own beliefs onto the patient as they may find it offensive, even if you mean well. Also death and dying carry significant spiritual meaning to all people, not just those who practise a particular faith. Muslims and Jewish people often visit in large numbers as it is considered a duty to visit the sick. The Muslim family will wish to pray or quote from the Qur'an beside or as near to the patient as possible. If no Muslim family members are available when a patient is dying, the Islamic Council should be informed so that spiritual support can be provided. Personal care should be carried out by a person of the same sex. For Hindus the family will wish to provide personal care. In Islam death is the beginning of eternal life; therefore the family may appear calm and accepting, which may seem unusual to non-Muslims. Hindus may shriek when mourning.

If possible, post-mortems should be avoided for Muslims, whereas Hindus will wish to be cremated as soon as possible after death. If a Muslim patient is in a coma or after death, they should preferably face Mecca, roughly towards the southeast in Ireland. (Afridi, 2005; McGarry, 2007). Due to a predominantly Roman Catholic population, the Christian and Catholic faiths have, for many years, been accommodated more readily in the Irish healthcare system. The local priest and chaplain are often readily accessible and Catholic Mass and communion is available weekly in most institutions. The family of a Catholic patient may wish to pray or have Mass said at their bedside by the priest. This can bring huge comfort, prior to and after death. The Travelling community also have their own beliefs about death and dying. This is a small representation of Ireland's growing diverse population. To provide spiritual care it is important to find out as much information as possible from the patient or their family. This will help you care for them appropriately before and after death.

Think about your own culture: what practices or rituals are important before or after death?

Bereavement

When a person dies, even if it is expected, the feeling of loss and sorrow felt by their loved ones can be overwhelming. In specialist palliative care units, bereavement support for the family begins at an early stage before their loved one has died. The Irish Hospice Foundation provides bereavement support services. It is an essential component of palliative care and should be provided in any area where palliative care is provided. It is essential to grieve and mourn the loss felt. Grief can manifest itself in many ways. The person will often experience feelings of anger, guilt, depression and shock, to name but a few. They may have physical problems, e.g. chest tightness, difficulty swallowing and lethargy. Although normal, if these feelings are interfering with the person's ability to function they should be treated by their GP. Worden suggests that the bereaved person must go through what he describes as the 'tasks of mourning' (Worden, 1991). The mourning process does not have a time limit, but it is necessary for the person to acknowledge their loss and to find life bearable again. They must first accept the reality of their loss. This acceptance can be very difficult, especially in sudden death. Often you may find the family returning to the place of death, or not returning to collect belongings, as it may represent acceptance of the person being gone. The family may also have many questions which need to be answered; these must be referred to the nurse in charge. They must also work through the pain grief causes. This emotional pain can manifest itself physically; it is traumatic for the person and they often feel it will never go away. Not everyone will experience the same level of pain, even within the same family people grieve differently. Suppressing this pain means the person will carry it through their life. They must also adjust to an environment in which the deceased is missing. This can take a considerable length of time and often depends on their relationship to the deceased. It can mean having to take on additional responsibilities as a parent or provider, or it can mean letting go of being a full-time carer. There are agencies and organisations that can help, and it is important to provide this information where appropriate. Even a simple information leaflet is enough to show the person they do not have to do this on their own. Finally they must find a safe place for the deceased in their emotions. This is where the bereaved can talk fondly about the deceased without finding it too emotional; they can cope with their memories and start to think about the future. It does not mean they have forgotten about their loved one, but life has become bearable, and hope and meaning have returned.

Palliative Care for Children

This differs from adult palliative care as many children live with life-limiting conditions and can live for a long time. They will mostly be cared for at home with support from the GP, public health nurse and specialist palliative care team. Paediatric hospitals will also have specialist teams who care for the children when they are in hospital and in some areas provide outreach care when the child has returned home.

Assignment Guidelines

FETAC LEVEL 5 PALLIATIVE CARE SUPPORT MODULE: D20170

For readers undertaking the above module, either as a stand-alone module or as part of their overall award, this chapter has been written with you in mind. There are two assignments required to complete the module.

Learner record weighting: 70%

Your learner record is an account of your experiences of caring for the dying patient and their family. The purpose of this is to help you reflect on your experiences. Reflection gives you the opportunity to learn about your communication and interpersonal skills, your strengths and weaknesses and how you can develop in your role as a healthcare assistant. Some of the questions throughout this chapter will have allowed you to explore these areas and can be useful when compiling your learner record.

Assignment weighting: 30%

The assignment gives you an opportunity to focus on one area of palliative care, and learn more about it. You need to investigate the topic area, and identify how it affects the patient and their family. Identify the treatments available to relieve symptoms experienced by the patient. Conclude the effect this care has on the patient and their family and the role of healthcare staff in managing this. Identify the communication and interpersonal skills required to deal sensitively and appropriately with the patient and their family.

CARE OF PEOPLE WITH MENTAL ILLNESS
Anna Maria Doyle

What is Mental Health?; What is Mental Illness?; Causes and Treatment of Mental Illness; The Most Common Types of Mental Illness; The Mental Healthcare Team; Role of the Healthcare Assistant; Holistic Care

Introduction

Mental illness has been recognised worldwide for thousands of years. Up to the late eighteenth century, the causes and treatment of mental illness were based on superstition, demons and witchcraft (Davies and Janosik, 1991). Today, as a result of advances in science, education and ongoing research, there is a better understanding of mental illness and the most effective way to treat it. However, there is still a stigma attached to mental illness and it is often regarded as a major affliction by society (Morrison-Valfre, 2005). Mental illness is prevalent worldwide and it is estimated that approximately 400 million people are suffering from various types of mental illness and that one out of every four persons visiting a health service suffers from some type of mental illness (WHO, 2001). As a HCA, you are very likely to care for people with a mental illness, even if you do not work in a facility which specialises in this type of care. The most common types of mental illnesses are depression, anxiety and schizophrenia. The terms 'mental illness' and 'mental health' are often used in the same context, but they do not mean the same thing and mental health is often regarded as the opposite to mental illness because it implies a healthy and illness-free mind.

What is Mental Health?

The World Health Organisation states that mental health is 'a state of wellbeing in which every individual realises his or her own potential, can cope with the normal stresses of life, can work productively and fruitfully, and is able to make a contribution to her or his community'. According to Mental Health Ireland (2007), mental health is involved with many aspects of our lives including:

- How we feel about ourselves
- How we feel about others
- How we are able to meet the demands of life.

Mental health is more than the absence of mental illness; it is about maintaining a state of emotional balance in our lives. People who are mentally healthy can use coping and defence mechanisms to enable them to adjust to the stress of everyday life, for example financial worries or worries about losing your job. These mechanisms usually relieve the stress and your emotional balance stabilises again.

What is Mental Illness?

Mental illness, or mental disorder, is a term used to refer to all the different types of mental illness, including disorders of thought, mood and behaviour.

The Mental Health Act, 2001 defines mental illness as 'a state of mind of a person which affects the person's thinking, perceiving, emotion or judgment and which seriously impairs the mental function of the person to the extent that he or she requires care or medical treatment in his or her own interest or in the interest of other persons.' To be classified as a mental illness, the condition must cause distress; it must be sustained or ongoing and result in a reduced ability to function in some or all aspects of a person's life.

People with mental illness may have difficulty coping with emotions such as stress and anger, they may be unable to handle family or financial responsibilities and they may have problems with relationships.

Terms currently in use to describe people with mental illness include 'patients', 'clients', 'consumers', 'people with mental illness' and 'service users'. According to a report by the Department of Health and Children (2006), the term 'service user' was chosen as the preferred term and is the one most commonly used in community care. The term 'patient' was not acceptable to the majority of people with mental illness as they felt that most of their treatment and interventions were provided in the community. In the hospital setting the term 'client' is still used, and is currently used in the module descriptors for the healthcare assistant programme; therefore it is the term I have used throughout this chapter. Whatever term we use to describe clients in need of mental healthcare, there is still a certain amount of stigma attached to mental illness. The World Health Organisation (2001) stated that a stigma can be defined as 'a mark of shame, disgrace or disapproval which results in an individual being shunned or rejected by others'. Research shows that in Ireland a stigma still exists in relation to mental health (NOSP, 2007), and six out of ten adults who participated in the research stated that they would not want people knowing about it if they themselves were experiencing mental health problems. People tend to use stereotypes and labels when describing someone with a mental illness and it is a sign of social unacceptability. Society tends not to give the same acceptance to mental illness as they do to physical illness. Fortinash & Holoday Worret (2004) suggest that the general public lack understanding about mental illness. They fear individuals who demonstrate symptoms of mental illness and sometimes equate it with violence. Recent evidence has found that only a small percentage of people with mental illness are violent (Morrison-Valfre, 2005). This type of stigma is unhelpful and can result in discrimination. It can increase feelings of loneliness and despair, which add to the burden of having to suffer and bear the symptoms of mental illness. Stigma against people with mental illness must be eradicated if they are to be treated fairly in the healthcare system. The following are some of the key principles suggested by the WHO (2001) to reduce the stigma associated with mental illness:

- Provide accurate information on the causes, prevalence, course and effects of mental illness.
- Talk openly about mental illness in the community.
- Provide support and treatment services that enable persons suffering from a mental illness to participate in all aspects of community life.
- Ensure the existence of legislation to reduce discrimination in the workplace, in access to health and social community services.
- Counteract the negative stereotypes and misconceptions surrounding mental illness by campaigning in the workplace, the media and the general public to break down the myths associated with mental illness.

There are voluntary support groups that offer information talks to companies and businesses throughout Ireland to educate the workforce about the nature and effects of mental illness. The Health Service Executive (HSE) offices can provide details of these support services. All healthcare staff should be aware of the effects of stigma on the individual with mental illness and we should avoid labelling or stereotyping them.

Causes and Treatment of Mental Illness

Mental illness has many different causes. Some types of mental illness, such as schizophrenia, are genetic, which means they run in families. Studies found that schizophrenia occurs more often in families where there is a parent, brother or sister with the disorder. Environmental factors are also thought to cause schizophrenia and other mental disorders. Complications during pregnancy or birth or exposure to viruses have been identified as risk factors. Chemical imbalances in the brain are also thought likely to cause some forms of mental illness. The treatment for mental illness varies according to the symptoms of the disorder, but it is usually a combination of medications and psychosocial therapy. Psychosocial therapies are designed to meet the specific needs of each client and involve personal therapy, rehabilitation, social skills training, behavioural therapy, family education and self-help groups (Morrison-Valfre, 2005). In conjunction with drug treatment, psychosocial therapy has been found to be very effective in assisting individuals to maintain the highest possible levels of daily functioning.

The Most Common Types of Mental Illness

There are several different types of mental illness and the most common types include anxiety disorders, depression and schizophrenia. This chapter provides the starting point for learning about these disorders and as a HCA it is important that you understand them in order to meet the needs of this client group. Nurses in your place of work can help you to identify some of these disorders and can explain the client's condition. This can help you to apply what you have learned about these conditions to your client. There may be books, articles or leaflets in your workplace that can provide further information and by increasing your knowledge you will be better able to understand the issues and difficulties affecting clients with mental illness.

Anxiety

Anxiety is a feeling of uneasiness, dread, helplessness and uncertainty. It is a normal emotional response to real or perceived threats or to something that is occurring in our lives that may cause us stress (Fortinash & Holoday Worrett, 2004). Anxiety is universal and can affect everyone, from children to the older adult. It is a normal part of life and mild anxiety can be positive in terms of getting us to focus, concentrate and to adapt, learn and grow from our experiences. According to Stuart and Laria (2005), 'Most of us have the capacity to tolerate mild anxiety and to use it consciously and constructively'. The majority of people deal with anxiety by using coping mechanisms that help decrease the stress or discomfort, e.g. physical exercise, relaxation or meditation.

Anxiety becomes an illness or disorder when an individual cannot call on their own coping methods to deal with the distress. The anxiety is usually excessive, meaning the person worries about numerous things and cannot concentrate on anything. It can last a long time, usually over six months (Stuart & Laria, 2005). There are different types of anxiety disorder such as phobias, panic disorders, obsessive compulsive disorder and generalised anxiety disorder, which is the type further discussed. This type of anxiety is regarded as severe in that it can be disabling and can cause many physical symptoms such as headaches, nausea, dizziness, fidgeting, sweating, loss of appetite, diarrhoea, increased heart rate and elevated blood pressure. The person may also experience psychological symptoms such as difficulty thinking clearly. They may become withdrawn and depressed. Emotional symptoms associated with severe anxiety are common and can include crying, feeling helpless, alone and insecure, or the person may become angry, argumentative or hostile. The treatment for anxiety disorders usually involves a combination of mental health therapies and medication. Initially the aim of treatment is to help the client to cope appropriately with their anxieties and eventually to prevent or minimise them.

DEPRESSION

At some time or other, everyone has felt somewhat depressed, but this feeling does not tend to last very long in healthy people. Depression is common and affects about 121 million people worldwide (WHO, 1997). According to AWARE (2007), it is estimated that over 400,000 people in Ireland experience depression. Depression is a mental state characterised by excessive sadness, loss of interest, disturbed sleep or appetite, and it can occur on several levels, from mild to severe depression (Stuart & Laria, 2005). Mild depression is short-lived and may occur as a result of life's disappointments or following a significant loss such as losing your job, financial or relationship difficulties or illness. The individual may complain of feeling let down or being disappointed, but the feelings usually subside when life begins to return to normal. In the short term the person may need medication or counselling to help them through their recovery.

Moderate and severe depression persists over a longer period of time and the individual may feel dejected, gloomy, drained of energy and find it hard to get through the day. They may have a negative outlook on life with recurrent thoughts of death and it is important to remember that depression always carries the risk of suicide. Therefore clients who are depressed are often admitted to hospital as they require a lot of care if suicide is to be prevented.

How would you know if a client in your care was suffering from depression?

Sometimes it is easy to tell if a client is depressed by their facial expression, posture and gestures. The person may be able to express in words their feelings of despair or guilt. It is easy to be empathetic towards this type of client and give emotional warmth and support. However, not all depressed people can voice their feelings and some may appear apathetic (lack interest), flat or emotionless and they may not communicate with you or respond to your questions. The absence of emotion may make it difficult for the client to express their feelings. Stuart & Laria (2005) advise that it may not be easy for healthcare workers to give emotional warmth and personal care to a client who is unresponsive and detached. Communication skills are important in caring for all clients with mental illness, but even more so in the client with depression, especially the unresponsive client. It is very important to familiarise yourself with the principles of communication and they are discussed in Chapter 5 of this book. Research shows that clients who recovered from depression greatly appreciated the efforts made by the healthcare staff who developed a rapport with them, even if the client themselves did not respond. The clients stated that they felt they were valued and it helped to increase feelings of self-worth (Stuart & Laria, 2005).

Depression can affect all age groups and, according to Morrison-Valfre (2005), 'mood disorders such as depression are increasing among children'. Depression is also common among older people and may go undiagnosed as older people may accept it as part of the ageing process. However, Phair (1999) states that depression is not a normal consequence of ageing and when it does occur it is more likely to be linked to a physical illness or it can be caused by a combination of physical, psychological and social factors. Grief, loss and bereavement are also significant factors in depression among older people (Hegge & Fischer, 2000; Wade, 1994).

MANIC DEPRESSION OR BIPOLAR DISORDER

Bipolar disorder (also called manic depression) is a disturbance of mood, in which elated or manic periods alternate with phases of depression (Morrison-Valfre, 2005). Some people experience long periods of normal functioning between attacks of depression or mania, while other people pass gradually from one phase to the other. The American Psychiatric Association (2000) defined mania as 'an abnormally and persistently elevated, expansive, or irritable mood'. The individual is elated and feels on top of the world. They are usually hyperactive and their speech may be very rapid and difficult to comprehend. They usually find it difficult to concentrate on any particular task and can easily become irritable or aggressive if they are not allowed to carry out their intentions. Clients with bipolar disorder are usually treated in hospital during the manic phase as there may be a serious danger to their physical health. The client is usually so overactive that it may be difficult to get them to take adequate nourishment or rest. They may become dehydrated as a result of their excessive activity and exhausted due to an inadequate diet and lack of sleep. Falls and other injuries are common during the manic phase as clients often lose control of their movements because of the hyperactivity, and proper safeguards must be in place to prevent this occurring (Kneisl et al., 2004). Treatment for mania consists of drug therapy and various other therapies such as counselling, which can assist clients in developing insight into their illness and help them to control some of the symptoms. Providing adequate rest and nourishment are also important aspects of the client's treatment.

SCHIZOPHRENIA

Schizophrenia is a severe chronic brain disorder and it affects about 24 million people worldwide, mostly in the 15–35 age group (WHO, 2001).

Most people with mental illness are able to function, change and adapt to their environment, but people with schizophrenia find it difficult to do so. The characteristics found in most clients with schizophrenia are a withdrawal of interest from everyday life and loss of contact with reality. This is referred to as 'psychosis'.

What are the symptoms of schizophrenia?

The symptoms of schizophrenia can be divided into two broad categories, positive and negative symptoms.

Positive symptoms include hallucinations and delusions.

A *hallucination* can be described as a false perception of something that is not really there; in other words a hallucination is something a person hears, sees, tastes, smells or feels. The person experiencing the hallucinations may hear sounds such as voices ordering them to do things or the voices may be talking about the individual. Hearing voices or auditory hallucinations are the most common type (Kneisl *et al.* 2004).

A *delusion* is a false personal belief held by the individual with schizophrenia and they will not alter their belief even if you explain or present proof that it is irrational. People with schizophrenia may have bizarre delusions, such as believing that the newscaster on television is specifically addressing them. They may also have delusions of persecution and the person may think that they are constantly being spied or that they are constantly being followed by someone who wishes to inflict harm on them (Kneisl *et al.* 2004).

Negative symptoms refer to reductions in normal emotional states and this means that the individual may lack emotion, interest or pleasure in everyday life. They may have difficulty when communicating with people as a disturbance of speech is common in schizophrenia. The individual may repeat similar sounding words, for example honey, money, sunny, or they may rapidly change topics several times while in conversation with people; this is referred to as flight of ideas (Morrison-Valfre, 2005). Individuals with schizophrenia often neglect basic hygiene and they may have an unkempt appearance. For this reason people may judge them as being lazy as it may not be obvious that the negative symptoms are part of a mental illness (Stuart & Laria, 2005).

Treatment for schizophrenia focuses on eliminating the symptoms of the illness. This involves drug therapy and psychosocial therapy, which deals with certain aspects of schizophrenia such as self-care, motivation, communication and socialisation. In the past people with schizophrenia were detained in mental institutions all their lives as they were seen as being violent and a threat to people in the community. In the past thirty years the outlook for people with schizophrenia has greatly improved. This is mostly due to antipsychotic medication. These drugs do not cure schizophrenia, but they do alleviate the positive and negative symptoms. When the client is stabilised on these drugs, they can usually attend school/college or work and live independent, satisfying lives in the community.

Schizophrenia and older people

While schizophrenia commonly affects the 15–35 year age group, research shows that it can occur in people in their forties and fifties (Peck, 2002). Older people with schizophrenia tend to become more withdrawn. They may still have the hallucinations and delusions of their younger years, but more than likely these symptoms will have decreased or disappeared (Morrison-Valfre, 2005).

The Mental Healthcare Team

In the past thirty years since the de-institutionalisation (the release of large numbers of mentally ill people into the community) of the psychiatric hospitals, there has been an increased awareness of the responsibility of the community to the mentally ill. There is a tendency to keep patients out of psychiatric hospitals, or to return them to the community as quickly as possible following a period in hospital. The vast majority of persons who avail of mental health services are treated in the community in outpatient settings, day hospitals, day centres and in their own homes. This is referred to as out-patient services. Within the community a greater understanding of the needs of the mentally ill is being developed, and, according to Stuart and Laria (2005), community care offers the best opportunity for retaining all that is best in the patient's adjustment. The goal is to prevent hospitalisation and support the individual in reaching their optimum level of functioning.

Whether the client receives treatment in hospital, referred to as in-patient services, or in the community, the general principles of care are the same and the aim of treatment is to help the client to learn new methods of adjustment to their illness. To achieve this, clients are cared for by various healthcare disciplines or healthcare teams, often referred to as the multidisciplinary team (MDT). The following are some of the members of the MDT who may be involved in providing care for a client with mental illness: The general practitioner (GP), psychiatrist, psychologist, social worker, psychiatric nurse, occupational therapist, HCA, psychotherapist and others, such as counsellors. The client's family and relatives are also part of the MDT as they may be able to provide further information on the client's disorder. It is usually the general practitioner (GP) that the client will initially visit to seek help for their disorder. The GP may prescribe medication or may refer the client to a specialist, for example a psychiatrist, as they specialise in mental disorders. The psychiatrist will assess the client and treat accordingly, usually in the community, or may advise admission to hospital if the client's symptoms are severe or disabling. The psychiatrist may refer the client to a clinical psychologist as they are trained in aspects of the assessment and treatment of mental illness and are involved in counselling therapy. The psychotherapist is another member of the MDT to whom the client can be referred and they provide treatment for mental disorders using different types of psychotherapy, which include behavioural, cognitive and crisis-intervention therapies (Morrison-Valfre, 2005). These therapies are tailored to meet the needs of the client and the psychotherapist may provide them on an individual basis or as part of group therapy. When the client has been assessed and a treatment plan has been established, the other members of the MDT play a central role in the client's care. The psychiatric nurse, in the hospital setting, plans, coordinates and integrates the multidisciplinary care delivery and evaluates the outcomes of the treatment plan for the client. The community psychiatric nurse is usually involved with the MDT in planning the discharge of the client back to the community and calls to their home or meets with them in day centres to ensure that they are coping with their environment and that they are following any treatment plan that may have been prescribed. The occupational therapist works in both the in-patient and out-patient setting and their role is to enable the client to reach their maximum level of function and independence. This can involve teaching the client self-help activities or assisting and preparing them to seek employment (Kneisl *et al.*, 2004).

The client's family may also need support and this is usually provided by a mental health social worker who will liaise with them and endeavour to help them to adapt to the client and their needs. Including families in the treatment process is vital and family members should be told as much about the illness as possible. The National Institute of Mental Health (2006) suggests that family members should be taught coping strategies and problem-solving skills to manage their ill relative effectively. The social worker may also liaise with the client's employer or other various services, for example community welfare officers or voluntary bodies, that can provide help with employment, accommodation and rehabilitation.

The multidisciplinary mental health team would not be complete without the client. The client is encouraged to take an active role in managing their illness but, depending on the severity of the client's disorder, this may not always be possible. A client requiring in-patient treatment may have lived through a period of tension and strain before admission and may not be capable of making decisions about their treatment; therefore the hospital must provide the environment to meet the needs of the client. Within the hospital environment all healthcare workers are governed by codes of ethics, which are a set of rules or values that define correct or proper conduct. Ethical principles involve treating the client equally, fairly and respectfully and providing treatment that is the most therapeutic for the client.

The multidisciplinary approach to caring for clients with a mental illness ensures that they are being provided with the best overall care and, as a HCA, you play a pivotal role in enhancing the quality of care for your clients.

The Role of the Healthcare Assistant

Caring for clients with mental illness is both challenging and rewarding. Under supervision of the registered nurse, the HCAs are involved in assessing and identifying clients' needs. Assessment is not a once-off activity, but is an ongoing process as clients' needs may change from day to day. It is very important to report any behavioural or physical changes in your clients' behaviour to the nurse immediately; this will ensure that clients are not suffering needlessly, but we also must always be aware of the risk of suicide. Clients with mental illness have a wide range of needs and to meet these needs they need to be assessed holistically.

Holistic Care

Holistic care is based on the concept of caring for the 'whole' person and taking all their individual needs into account. In the past healthcare was based on the traditional medical model which viewed illness as a pathological condition, meaning that something was 'wrong' with the client and a 'cure' had to be found to repair or return them to normal functioning (Morrison-Valfre, 2005). The medical model tended to focus on the person's physical health only. It did not regard other aspects, such as mental, emotional, social or spiritual, as being related or dependent on each other (Fortinash & Holoday-Worret, 2004). In recent years healthcare has begun to focus on a health-oriented model, which involves caring for the person from a physical, psychological, emotional, social and spiritual perspective, and this is referred to as holistic care. Holistic care places the client at the centre of their care, and they are assessed by the healthcare team to identify their strengths and abilities rather than their illness or disability. The client and the care providers work together to ensure that the client receives the services and treatment that is relevant and most important to them. Providing holistic care to clients with mental illness may be slow and difficult at times, as some clients may not be able to verbalise their needs or they may not be capable of making decisions about their care. Trust and empathy are principles of mental healthcare that are very important in terms of providing holistic care. Trust is the firm belief in the reliability and honesty of another person (Fortinash & Holoday-Worret, 2004). Many clients have experienced, in childhood, difficulties in some of their basic relationships. These difficulties have resulted in disturbed relationships with people in adult life. Therefore these clients may be suspicious of healthcare staff and may be unable to trust them. As caregivers we must make our clients aware that we will provide care for them in a safe and supportive manner and we will do no harm to them but will protect them. These principles are the responsibility of all healthcare staff, whether they are working in the community or in a hospital.

The specific care of each client depends on the nature of their illness, but whatever their diagnosis we, as healthcare staff, must accept them as they are and acknowledge their situation by empathising with them (Keltner *et al.*, 2003).

Empathy is the ability to understand the thoughts and emotions of another person. Empathy is often described as putting yourself in the other person's shoes in an attempt to understand the meaning and significance of that person's behaviour (Morrison-Valfre, 2005). We may not always like the client's behaviour, attitude or way of life, but we must accept it even if it may cause them harm. Therefore as healthcare providers we must be able to adapt to all types of clients, from the most depressed and helpless to the most excited and overactive. We must respect them and not pass judgment on them, regardless of how their behaviours or beliefs differ from our own. Morrison-Valfre (2005) stated that 'a holistic point of view and a focus on the positive encourage both care providers and the client to strive for success'. If clients see that you are willing to care for them as a 'whole' person rather than just their specific mental illness, it may be a first step towards their recovery.

Having read this chapter you will now be aware of the most common types of mental illness and also their signs and symptoms. Caring for a client with mental illness is undertaken by the multidisciplinary team and this approach is widely accepted as being fundamental to the proper care and support for this client group. Caring for clients with mental illness can be rewarding and challenging and care providers are expected to work hard for the welfare of their clients. Therefore it is important to take care of yourself. How you choose to do this is a matter of personal preference, but the important thing is that you do it.

Assignment Guidelines

FETAC LEVEL 5 CARE OF PEOPLE WITH MENTAL ILLNESS MODULE: D20179

There are two assignments and one skills demonstration required to complete this module.

Skills demonstration weighting: 60%

You are required to carry out a planned task/activity in your clinical area and you will be assessed by a registered nurse who will allocate you marks out of 50. Read the skills assessment sheet to become familiar with the range of practical skills you are expected to demonstrate. Gain consent from the client and remember to assess your client holistically beforehand in order to identify and meet their needs. Communication is an important aspect of this activity; remember to demonstrate observation and listening skills.

A written account of the task/activity must be submitted and this will be marked out of 10. This gives you a chance to reflect on the activity, what went well, what did not, and include recommendations for improvement.

Project weighting: 40%

This assignment gives you an opportunity to learn about a specific mental illness. However, it is important to remember that you are writing about a client whom you have cared for with a mental illness, so do not use all your word count on writing about the illness; it is important to focus on the client's needs. Again, as mentioned above it is important to assess your client holistically to identify their needs. The last section of the brief requires you to reflect on the knowledge you have gained as a result of carrying out this project and here you can discuss what you have learned about the illness and how the illness affects the client for whom you are caring. You can also discuss your responsibilities as a HCA and how they impact on caring for a client with mental illness.

REFERENCES

Afridi, Z. S. (2005) *Muslim Care Booklet*, Hospice Friendly Hospitals Programme, Ireland.

Age Action Ireland (2007) AGM.

Age Concern (2007) *Improving Services and Support for Older People with Mental Health Problems*.

American Psychiatric Association (2000) *Diagnostic and Statistical Manual of Mental Disorders*, 4th edition, Washington DC: The Association.

Andrews, M. & Boyle, J. (2003) *Transcultural Concepts in Nursing Care*, 4th edition, Philadelphia: Lippincott, Williams and Wilkins.

Andrews, M., Gidman, J., Humphreys, A. (1998) 'Reflection: does it enhance professional nursing practice?' *British Journal of Nursing* (7) 413–417.

AWARE (2007) *Helping to Defeat Depression*, Available: www.aware.ie/depression_p.htm (6 December 2007).

Barder, I., Slimmer, L., Lesage, J. (1994) 'Depression: on issues of control among elderly people in healthcare settings', *Journal of Advanced Nursing*, 20, 598–604.

Barnett, R. I., Shelton, F. E. (1997) 'Measurement of support surface efficacy: pressure', *Advances in Wound Care*, 10 (7) 21–25.

Basford, L., Slevin, O., Arets, J., Burgin, D., Gormley, K., Horton, R., James, J., Kirby, C., Maslen, B., Morle, K., Sinclair, M., Sines, D. & Vaessen, J. (1995) *Theory and Practice of Nursing in Integrated Approach to Patient Care*, Cheltenham: Stanley Thornes Ltd.

Beckmann, J.D. (1995) *Nursing Malpractice: Implications for Clinical Practice and Nurse Education*, Seattle: University of Washington Press.

Benner, P. & Tanner, C. (1987) 'How expert nurses use intuition', *American Journal of Nursing* 87 (1) 23–31.

Benner, P. & Wrubel, J. (1989) *The Primacy of Caring*, California: Addison-Wesley.

Bennie, A., Titchen, A. (1999) *Freedom to Practice: The Development of Patient-centred Nursing*, Oxford: Butterworth-Heinemann.

Benson, S. (ed.) (2000) *Handbook for Care Assistants: A Practical Guide to Caring for Elderly People*, 5th Edition. UK: Hawker Publications.

Braden, B, Bergstrom, N. (1987) 'A conceptual schema for the study of the aetiology of pressure sores', *Rehabilitation Nursing* 12(1), pp 8–12.

Bristol Royal Infirmary, Public inquiry into children's heart surgery at the Bristol Royal Infirmary, 1984–1995, (2001) *Learning from Bristol*, The Bristol Royal Infirmary.

British Institute of Learning Disability (BILD) (2000) *Managing Challenging Behaviour Trainer Pack*.

British Red Cross (1998) *Practical First Aid*, London: Dorling Kindersley.

Brooker, C., Nicol, M. (eds.) (2005) *Nursing Adults – The Practice of Caring*, Edinburgh: Mosby.

Census: www.cso.ie/census 2006.

College of Marin 'Barriers to Effective Communication' http://www.marin.edu/buscom/index_files/page0007.htm (accessed 15 December 2007).

Commission for Healthcare Audit and Inspection (2006) *Joint Investigation into the Provision of Services for People with Learning Disabilities*, Cornwall Partnership NHS Trust.

Conway, N. & Donoghue, S. (2003) *Core Themes for Care Assistants*, Oxon UK: Radcliff Medical Press.

Cooper, S.A. (2003) 'Classification and assessment of psychiatric disorders in adults with learning disabilities', *Psychiatry* 2 (8) 12–16.

Covey, S.R. (1992), *Principle-Centred Leadership*, New York: Free Press.

David, J.A., Chapman, E. & Lockett, B. (1983) *An Investigation of Current Methods Used in Nursing for the Care of Patients with Established Pressure Sores*, Harrow: Nursing practice research unit.

Davies, J. L., & Janosik, E. H. (1991) *Mental Health and Psychiatric Nursing*, Boston: Jones and Bartlett Publishers.

Davis, S., Slack, R., Larker, S., Philip, I. (1998) 'The educational preparation of staff in nursing homes: relationship to patient autonomy', *Journal of Advanced Nursing* 29 (1) 208–217.

Department of Health and Children (1998) *Report of the Commission on Nursing – A Blueprint for the Future*, Dublin: Government Publications.

Department of Health and Children (2000) *The National Health Promotion Strategy 2000–2005*, Dublin: Department of Health and Children.

Department of Health and Children (2001) *Mental Health Act (2001)* Available:http://www.mhcirl.ie/act/mentalhealthact.pdf (6 December 2007).

Department of Health and Children (2001) *Report of the National Advisory Committee on Palliative Care*, Ireland.

Department of Health and Children (2001) *The Health Strategy, Quality and Fairness: A Health System for You*, Dublin: Government Publications.

Department of Health and Children (2004) *Final Report of the Review Group on Health Service Staff*, Dublin: Government Publications.

Department of Health and Children (Nursing Policy Division, 2000), *Report of the Effective Utilisation of Professional Skills for Nurses and Midwives*, Ireland.

Department of Health and Children, Ireland (2006) *A Vision for Change*, Report of the Expert Group on Mental Health Policy.

Department of Health and Social Services (1972) *Report of the Committee on Nursing* (Briggs), London: HMSO.

DeVito, J. A. (2004), *The Interpersonal Hand Book,* 10th edition, Boston: Pearson Education.

Dictionary of Nursing (2002), 18th Edition, UK: Churchill Livingstone.

Douglas, A. & O'Neill, S. (2006) *The Essential Work Experience Handbook*, 2nd edition, Ireland: Gill & Macmillan.

Dustagheer, A., Harding & J., McMahon, C. (eds.) (2005) *Knowledge to Care: A Handbook For Care Assistants*, 2nd Edition, Oxford: Blackwell Science Ltd.

End of Life Care (2007) *Debate of the Age, Health & Care Study Group* (1999) Volume 1 (1).

Erickson, L. & Williams-Evans, S. A. (2000) 'Attitudes of emergency nurses regarding patient assaults', *Journal of Emergency Nursing* 26, 282–288.

Ewles, L. & Simnett, I. (1999) *Promoting Health* (4th edition), London: Balliere Tindall.

Finnema, E. J., Dassen, T. & Halfens, R. (1994), 'Aggression in psychiatry: a qualitative study focusing on the characterisation and perception of patient aggression by nurses working on psychiatric wards'. *Journal of Advanced Nursing* 19, 1088–1095.

Flanagan, M. (1993) 'Predicting pressure sore risk', *Journal of Wound Care*, 2 (4), 215–218.

Forbes, S. B., (1994) 'Hope: an essential human need in the elderly', *Journal of Gerontological Nursing*, June 5.

Fortinash, K. M., Holoday Worret, P. A. (2004) *Psychiatric Mental Health Nursing* (3rd edition), Missouri: Mosby.

Gibbs, G. (1988) *Learning by Doing: A Guide to Teaching and Learning Methods*, Oxford: Oxford Further Education Unit.

Globalisation Guide (2006) 'What is Globalisation?' www.globalisationguide.org.

Gott, M., Seymour, J., Bellamy, G., Clark, D., & Ahmedzai, S. (2004) 'Older people's views about home as a place of care at the end of life', *Palliative Medicine*, Vol. 18, No. 5, 460–467 DOI: 10.1191/0269216304pm889oa © 2004 SAGE Publications.

Government Publications (1989) *The Safety, Health and Welfare at Work Act 1989*. Acts of the Oireachtas (online). Available 7 December 2007: http://acts.oireachtas.ie/zza7y1989.1.html.

Government Publications (1996) *Guide to Fire Safety in Existing Nursing Homes and Similar Type Premises*, Irish Fire Services (online). Available 7 Dec 2007: http://www.irishfireservices.com/pages/publications.htm.

Government Publications (2005) *The Safety, Health and Welfare at Work Act 2005*. Acts of the Oireachtas (online). Available 7 December 2007: http://www.oireachtas.ie/viewdoc.asp?DocID=4305.

Gross, R. D. (1987) *Psychology: The Science of Mind and Behaviour*, London: Edward Arnold.

Grubbs, P. A. & Blasband, B. A. (2005) *Long-term Care Nursing Assistant*, 3rd Edition, New Jersey, USA: Julie Levin Alexander.

Health Information and Quality Authority (Aug 2007). *Draft National Quality Standards for Residential Care Setting for Older People – A Consultation Document,* Information and Quality Authority.

Health Information and Quality Authority (March 2008). *The National Quality Standards for Residential Care Settings for Older People in Ireland.* Information and Quality Authority.

Health Service Executive 2006, *Report on the High Level Group on Healthcare Assistants – Regarding the Implementation of the Healthcare Assistant Programme,* Ireland.

Health Services Executive (2007) *National Review of the Role of the Healthcare Assistant in Ireland*, www.skillproject.ie.

Healthy Ageing Project 2007, *A Challenge for Europe* (Short Version), Stockholm www.healthyageing.nu.

Hegge, M. and Fischer, C. (2000) 'Grief responses of senior and elderly widows: practice implications', *Journal of Gerontological Nursing* 26 (2) 35–43.

Heidric, R. (2005), *Senior Fitness: The Diet and Exercise Program for Maximum Health and Longevity*, New York: Lantern Books.

Higgs, P., MacDonald, L., Ward, M. (1992) 'Responses to the institute among elderly patients in hospital long-stay care', *Social Science and Medicine* 35 (3) 287–293.

Howard, H. (2000) *The Care Assistant's Handbook*, London: Age Concern.

Irish Hospice Foundation (2004): *A Nationwide Survey of Public Attitudes and Experiences Regarding Death and Dying*. Baseline study on the provision of hospice/specialist palliative care services in Ireland 2005. www.hospice-foundation.ie, Dublin.

Irish Nurses Organisation (2003) *Guidelines on the Use of Restraint in the Care of the Older Person*.

Jansen, G., Dassen, T. & Moorer, P. (1997) 'The perception of aggression', *Scandinavian Journal of Caring Sciences* 11, 51–55.

Jarvis, P. (1992) 'Reflecting practice and nursing', *Nurse Education Today* 12, 174–181.

Keeney, S. Hasson, F. & McKenna, H. (2005) 'Healthcare assistants: the views of managers of healthcare agencies on training and employment', *Journal of Nursing Management* 13, 83–92.

Keltner, N. L., Schwecke, L. H. & Bostrom, C. E. (2003) *Psychiatric Nursing*, 4th edition, Missouri: Mosby.

Kennedy, Maureen, Mini Thesis. 'Workplace Violence: An exploratory study into nurse's interpretations and responses to violence and aggression'.

Knapp, M. and Hall, J. (2002) *Nonverbal Behaviour in Human Interaction* (5th edition), New York: Wadsworth.

Kneisl, C. R., Skodol Wilson, H. & Trigoboff, E. (2004) *Contemporary Psychiatric-Mental Health Nursing*, New Jersey: Pearson Prentice Hall.

Kolb, D. A. (1984) *Experiential Learning Experience as a Source of Learning and Development*, New Jersey: Eaglewood Cliffs.

Kubler-Ross, E. (1970) *On Death and Dying*, London: Tavistock/Routledge.

Lewin, K. (1947) 'Frontier in group dynamics: social planning and action research'. *Human Relations* 1 (1) 143–153.

Lunn, P., Doyle, N. & Hughes, G. (2007) *Occupational Employment Forecasts 2012: FÁS/ESRI Manpower Forecasting Studies Report No. 12*, ESRI August.

McGarry, P. 'When modesty is an obligation', *The Irish Times*, 10 July 2007.

McKenna, Keeney, S. & Hasson, F. (2003) *Investigation of the Education Provision for Healthcare Assistants*, Dublin: Department of Health and Children.

McMahon, C., Isaacs, R. (1997) *Care of the Older Person: A Handbook for Care Assistants*, Oxford: Blackwell Science.

Marais-Stein, S. (1998). 'The changing workplace', *Work Trauma Newsletter*.

Maryland, G. & McSherry, W. (1997) 'The reflective diary: an aid to practice-based learning', *Nursing Standard* 12, 13–15, 49–52.

Maslow, A. H. (1956) 'Self-actualising people: a study of psychological health', in Moustakas, C. E. (ed.) *The Self*, New York: Harper Row.

Mathieson, V., Sivertsen, L., Foreman, M. D. & Cronin-Stubbs, D. (1994) 'Acute confusion: nursing interventions in older people', *Orthopaedic Nursing* 13 (2) 21–28.

Mental Health Ireland (2007) Available: http://mentalhealthireland.ie/index.php (9 December 2007)

Mental Health Ireland, 'Supporting Positive Mental Health Communication', http://www.mentalhealthirelan.ie/information_supplement (accessed 30 July 2007).

Miller, M. P. (1991) 'Factors promoting wellness in the aged person: an ethnographic study', *Advances in Nursing Science*, 13 (4) 38–43.

Morrison, P. & Burnard, P. *Caring and Communicating*, Hampshire: Macmillan.

Morrison, R. S. & Meier D. (2003) *Geriatric Palliative Care*, Oxford University Press.

Morrison-Valfre, M. (2005) *Foundations of Mental Healthcare*, 3rd edition, Missouri: Mosby.

National Council for Vocational Awards, FETAC Work Experience Module Descriptor (2001).

National Institute for Clinical Excellence (2003) 'Infection control: prevention of healthcare-associated infection in primary and community care' (online). Available 2 December 2007: www.nice.org.uk.

National Institute of Mental Health (2006) Available: http://www.nimh.nih.gov/ publicat/schizoph.cfm (2 September 2007).

National Office for Suicide Prevention (2007). *Mental Health in Ireland: Awareness and Attitudes*, Health Service Executive.

Nazarko, L. (2000) *NVQs in Nursing and Residential Care Homes*, 2nd Edition, Oxford: Blackwell Science.

Newton, C. (1991) *The Roper Logan Tierney Model in Action*, London: Macmillan.

O'Connell, P. J. & Russell, H. (2005) *Workplace Equality Policies, Flexible Working Arrangements and the Quality of Work*. ESRI Dublin.

O'Rourke, M. & Bird, L. (2001) *Risk Management in Mental Health: A Practical Guide to Individual Care and Community Safety*, UK: The Mental Health Foundation.

Oleson, M., Heading, C., Shadick, K. M., Bistodeau, J. A. (1994) 'Quality of life in long-stay institutions in England: nurse and resident perceptions', *Journal of Advanced Nursing* 20, 23–32.

Pang, S. M. & Wong, T. K. (1998) 'Predicting pressure-sore risk with the Norton, Braden, and Waterlow scales in a Hong Kong Hospital', *Nursing Research* Vol. 47, No.3 pp.147–143.

Peck, R. L. (2002) 'Not just a young person's disorder', *Behavioural Health Management*, 22 (2) 29.

Phair, L. (1999) 'Mental Health', in Heath, H. & Schofield, I. (eds.) *Healthy Ageing: Nursing Older People*. London: Mosby.

Prasher, V. P. (2003) 'Psychiatric morbidity in adults with Down's syndrome', *Psychiatry* 2 (8) 21–24.

Pulliam, J. (2001) *The Nursing Assistant: Acute, Sub-acute and Long-term Care*, 3rd edition, New Jersey: Pulliam.

Reid, B. (1993) '"But we're doing it already!" – exploring a response to the concept of reflective practice in order to improve its facilitation'. *Nurse Education Today*.

Roper, N., Logan, W. & Tierney, A.(1990) *The Elements of Nursing: A Model of Nursing Based on a Model of Living*, 3rd edition, London: Churchill Livingstone.

Royal College of Nursing (2005) 'Good practice in infection prevention and control: guidance for nursing staff' (online) Available 9 December 2007: http://www.rcn. org.uk/_data/assets/pdf_file/0003/78654/002741.pdf.

Saunders, C. (1976b) 'Care of the dying –1' – The problem of euthanasia', *Nursing Times* (1 July 1972) (26) 1003–5.

Scottish Intercollegiate Guidelines Network (2000). 'Control of pain in patients with cancer', www.sign.ac.uk.

Scrutton, S. (1989) *Counselling for Older People: A Creative Response to Ageing*, London: Edward Arnold.

Shannon, M. *et al.* (2001) 'Effective utilisation of professional skills of nurses and midwives', *Report of the Working Group*, Nursing Policy Division, Brunswick Press, Dublin: Department of Health and Children.

Shephard, R. (1990) 'The scientific basis of exercising for the very old', *Journal American Geriatric Society*, (38) 62–65.

Soams, S. 'Therapeutic Communication' home page, circle time resources' links Steve http://www.portables1.ngfl.gov.uk (accessed 14 December 2007).

Spokes, K., Bond, K., Lowe, T., Jones, J., Illingworth, P., Brimblecombe, N. & Wellman, N. (2002) 'HOVIS – the Hertfordshire/Oxfordshire violent incident study', *Journal of Psychiatric and Mental Health Nursing* 9, 199–209.

St John Ambulance, St Andrew's Ambulance Association, *The British Red Cross (2002) First Aid Manual*, London: Dorling Kindersley Limited.

Stuart, G. W., Laria, M. T. (2005) *Principles and Practice of Psychiatric Nursing*, 8th edition, Missouri: Elsevier Mosby.

Sully, P. & Dallas, J. *Essential Communication Skills for Nursing*, London: Mosby.

The Health and Safety Authority (1998) *Caring with Minimal Lifting: A Safety and Health Guide for those who Care for Patients*. Dublin: Health and Safety Authority.

The Health and Safety Authority (2001) *Report of the Advisory Committee on the Health Services Sector*. Dublin: Health and Safety Authority.

The Health and Safety Authority (2002) 'Guidelines on first aid at places of work' (online) Available 8 December 2007: http://publications.hsa.ie/index.asp?docID=97.

The Health and Safety Authority (2004) 'Obligatory safety signs' (online) Available 8 December 2007: http://publications.hsa.ie/index.asp?docID=162.

The Health and Safety Authority (2005) 'A short guide to the Safety, Health and Welfare at Work Act' (online) Available 8 December 2007: http://publications.hsa.ie/index.asp?locID=18&docID=152.

The Health and Safety Authority (2005) *Guidance on the Management of Manual Handling in the Workplace*, Dublin: Health and Safety Authority.

The Health Service Executive (2007) 'Say no to infection: infection control action plan – The prevention and control of healthcare-associated infections in Ireland' (online) Available 8 December 2007: http://www.hse.ie/en/NewsEvents/News/HCAI/.

Torrence, C. (1983) *Pressure Sores: Aetiology Treatment and Prevention*, Beckenham: Croom Helm.

Wade L. & Waters K. (1996) *A Textbook of Gerontological Nursing*, London: Balliere Tindall.

Wade, B (1994) 'Depression in older people: a study', *Nursing Standard*, 8, 29–35.

Watson, M. & Lucas, C. (2003) *Adult Palliative Care Guidelines*, Southwest London, Surrey, West Sussex and Hampshire Cancer Networks.

Wigglesworth, N. (2003) 'The use of protective isolation', *Nursing Times* Vol 99, no 26, 26–27.

Windmill, V. (1996) *Caring for the Elderly*, Essex: Addison Wesley Longman.

Worden, J. W. (1991) *Grief Counseling and Grief Therapy: A Handbook for the Mental Health Practitioner*, 2nd edition, New York: Springer.

World Health Organisation (1990) *Cancer Pain Relief and Palliative Care: Report of Expert Committee*.

World Health Organisation (2001) *Mental Health in the WHO European Region*, fact sheet EURO/03/03   Available: www.who.int/mediacentre/factsheets/fs03/print.html (December 2007).

York, V. (2002) 'Using protective clothing', *Nursing Times* 98: 52   http://www.nursing times.net.

Zernike, W. & Sharpe, P. (1998) 'Patient aggression in a general hospital setting: do nurses perceive it to be a problem?' *International Journal of Nursing Practice* 4, 126–133.

INDEX

abuse, 125
Acquired Immune Deficiency Syndrome
    (AIDS), 137
Active Retirement Association, 101, 102
activities of living (ALs), 15, 21–2
    care skills, 32–49
    fundamental needs, 26–7
acupuncture, 11
Advisory Committee on the Health Services
    Sector, 65–6
advocacy, 20–1
Age & Opportunity, 114
Age Action Ireland, 3, 102, 114
Age and Opportunity, 102, 103
Age Concern, 122
ageing
    effects of, 100
    healthy, 96, 101–2
    process of, 97–100
ageism, 102–3
aggression, management of, 125–6
alcohol, 67
Alzheimer's Association, 121
Alzheimer's Society of Ireland, 114
American Psychiatric Association, 156
Andrews, M. and Boyle, J., 77
anxiety, 34, 154–5
application forms, 91
aromatherapy, 11
arthritis, 106
autonomy, 10
AWARE, 155

barrier nursing, 60
Basford, L. et al., 66
bed bath, 40–1
Benson, S., 54
bereavement, 148–9

challenging behaviour, 122
bipolar disorder, 156
body language, 73–4
body temperature, 42
Bord Altranais, An, 125
bowel incontinence, 39
breathing problems, 35–6
British Institute of Learning Disabilities
    (BILD), 116
Brooker, C. & Nicol, M., 60

cancer, 137
cardiovascular accident, 106–7
care settings, 2, 113–14
care skills, 3, 4, 32–49
    breathing problems, 35–6
    communication, 34–5
    controlling body temperature, 42
    dying, 45–6
    eating and drinking, 36–7
    elimination, 37–9
    expressing sexuality, 44–5
    mobilising, 42–3
    personal hygiene, 39–42
    pressure-sore prevention, 46–9
    safe environment, 33–4
    sleep, 45
    work and recreation, 43–4
care support, 3, 8–31
    advocacy, 20–1
    confidentiality, 16–17
    difficult clients, 13
    diversity awareness, 9–11
    fundamental needs, 25–7
    partnership approach, 11–12
    privacy/dignity/individuality, 17–20
    promoting wellness, 14
    relating to clients, 8–9

care support, *continued*
 social relationships, 12–13
 vulnerable/confused clients, 14–16
Certificate in Healthcare Support (FETAC
 Level 5), 1, 3, 5
challenging behaviour, 6, 116–32
 causes of, 118–22
 communication, 127–8
 definition of, 116–17
 identification at early stage, 128–31
 legal considerations, 131
 safe environment, 127
children, palliative care for, 149
chronic illness, 105–7
chronic obstructive pulmonary disease, 106
circulatory system, ageing, 98
Clark, 66
clients, relating to, 8–9
cognitive impairment, 108–9
communication, 3, 5, 69–79
 barriers to, 75
 care skills, 34–5
 challenging behaviour, 127–8
 diversity awareness, 9–10
 and interpersonal skills, 70–1
 learning to communicate, 78–9
 methods of, 71–5
 overcoming barriers, 75–6
 palliative care, 142–3
 process of, 69–70
 social needs, 43–4
 therapeutic communication, 76–8
community healthcare assistants, 2
complementary therapies, 11
confidentiality, 16–17
confused clients, 14–16, 33
Covey, S.R., 69
cultural considerations (terminal care), 148
curriculum vitae (CV), 86, 89–90

Data Protection Act 1988, 92
Data Protection Act (Amendment) Act 2003,
 92
death, rituals of, 11, 148

delusions, 157
dementia, 109–11
dentures, cleaning, 42
dependency, 22, 32
depression, 155–6
diet, 67
 diversity awareness, 10
 older persons, 111–13
difficult clients, 13
digestive system, ageing, 98–9
dignity, protection of, 17–18, 18
disabilities, people with, 3, 4
diversity awareness, 9–11
 communication, 9–10
 dietary needs, 10
 family involvement, 10–11
 religious values, 10
Draft National Quality Standards, 4
dressing, 39–40
drugs, 67
Drumm, Professor Brendan, 3
dying, 6. *see also* palliative care support
 care skills, 45–6
 stages of grief, 139–41

e-mail, 72–3
eating and drinking, 36–7
Economic and Social Research Institute
 (ESRI), 96
elimination, 37–9
emotional needs, 35
employee, general duties of, 51
employer, general duties of, 51
employment legislation, 91–2
employment opportunities, 81–2
endocrine system, ageing, 99
environment, safe, 33–4, 127
environmental factors
 challenging behaviour, 119
Equality Act, 2004, 92
Equality Authority, 92, 102
equality legislation, 91–2
exercise, 67
exploitation, 125

eyesight, failing, 33

faecal evacuation, assisted, 37–8
faecal incontinence, 39
'Fair Deal, A,' 114
family involvement
    diversity awareness, 10–11
    palliative care, 142–3, 145–6
Farrell, 124
fax, 72–3
Finnema, E.J. *et al.*, 119
fire prevention, 55–7
first aid, 62–4
first-aid kit, 63
food, 36–7
Fortinash, K.M. and Holoday Worret, P.A.,
    153
Further Education and Training Council
    (FETAC), 81

Gibbs, G., 28
Gill and Macmillan, 68
globalisation, 80–1
Go for Life, 102
goals, setting, 85–6
grief, stages of, 139–41
Gross, R.D., 8

hallucinations, 157
hand washing, 59–60
Harney, Mary, 3
hazards, 52–3
Health and Children, Department of, 66–7,
    114, 152
Health and Safety Authority (HSA), 53, 55,
    64, 65
Health Commission, 121
Health Service Executive (HSE), 2, 81, 153
healthcare assistants (HCA), 1–2, 1–3
    community healthcare assistants, 2
healthcare associated infections (HCAI), 57
healthy ageing
    definition of, 96
    promotion of, 101–2

Healthy Ageing — A Challenge for Europe, 102
hearing, impaired, 33, 108
hierarchy of needs, 25–6
Hinduism, 148
HIV, 67
holistic care, 160–1
home-care packages, 3
homeopathic treatments, 11
hospice care. *see* palliative care support
human growth and development, 22–5
    fundamental needs, 25–7
human touch, 44–5
hygiene, personal, 39–42

inactivity, 42–3
    complications of, 43
incontinence, 38–9
individuality, protection of, 17–20
infection control, 4–5, 33–4, 57–62
    barriers, 58–60
    causes, 57–8
    spread, 58
interactional factors
    challenging behaviour, 119
interpersonal skills
    and communication, 70–1
interview skills, 91–2
intimacy, 44
Irish Hospice Foundation, The, 114, 149
Irish Senior Citizens Parliament, 114
Islam, 148
isolating patients, 60–1

Jarvis, P., 27
Jewish community, 148

Kinsella, Joseph, 68
Knapp, M. and Hall, J., 73–4
knowledge, implementing, 30–1
Kubler-Ross, Dr Elizabeth, 134, 139–42

last offices, 147–8
legal considerations, 131
letter of application, 87–8

life stages, 22–5
listening, 71–2

manic depression, 156
manual handling, 64–6
Marais-Stein, S., 124
Maslow, Abraham, 25–6
Mathieson, V. *et al.*, 14
memory loss, 33, 108–9
men, and privacy, 18
mental health, 6–7
  definition of, 151–2
Mental Health Act, 2001, 152
Mental Health Ireland, 151–2
mental illness, 6–7, 151–62
  care team, 158–9
  causes and treatment of, 153–4
  challenging behaviour, 121–2
  common types of, 154–8
  definitions, 151–3
  role of HCA, 160–1
micro-organisms, 57–8
mobilising, 42–3
Model of Nursing (1980), 26
Morrison-Valfre, M., 156
Motor Neurone Disease, 137
MRSA, 4–5, 57
multidisciplinary team (MDT), 158–9
Multiple Sclerosis (MS), 137
musculoskeletel system, ageing, 98

National Advisory Committee on Palliative
    Care (NACPC), 138–9
National Health Promotion Strategy, 67
National Health Strategy, 1
National Institute of Clinical Excellence, 59
National Institute of Mental Health, 159
*National Quality Standards for Residential Care
    Settings for Older People in Ireland* (2008),
    1, 5, 116
neglect, 125
nervous system, ageing, 99
nutrition, 36–7

O'Brien, John, 125
'Older and Bolder' campaign, 114
Older People, Minister of State for, 97
older persons, care of, 3, 5–6, 96–115
  ageing process, 97–100
  care settings and services, 105, 113–14
  chronic illness, 105–7
  cognitive impairment, 106–11
  effects of ageing, 100
  needs of, 103–4
  nutritional needs, 111–13
  positive attitudes, 102–3
  promotion of healthy ageing, 101–2
  retirement preparation, 100–2
  role of HCA, 104–5
  schizophrenia, 158
oral hygiene, 41–2
oxygen/air, 35–6

pain control (palliative care), 143–4
palliative care, 6, 133–50
bereavement, 148–9
  care team, 137–9
  for children, 149
  communication skills, 142–3
  dying, 45–6
  history and definition, 135
  practice of, 135–6
  role of HCA in grief, 141–2
  settings, 136
  stages of grief, 139–41
  symptom management, 143–5
  terminal care, 145–9
partnership approach, 11–12
passivity, 19
Phair, L., 156
physical activity, 42–3
physical disability, 109
physiological factors
  challenging behaviour, 119–20
Prasher, V.P., 121
pressure sores, 4
  causes, 46–7
  classification of, 48–9

pressure points, 47
prevention, 46–9
privacy, protection of, 17–18
protective clothing, 60
protective isolation, 61
public health nurse (PHN), 2
pyschological cognitive factors
    challenging behaviour, 120–1

'Quality and Fairness, Health System for You'
    (NHS), 1
quality of life, 125–6

Red Cross, 62
reflective practice
    scenario, 28–30
    support care, 27–31
religious values, 10, 35, 77–8
reproductive system, ageing, 99–100
respiratory system, ageing, 98
restraints, 33
retirement, preparation for, 100–2
risk assessment, 52–3
    challenging behaviour, 123–6
    definition, 123
    risks to others, 123–4
    risks to self, 124
risk management
    challenging behaviour, 123–6
    definition, 123
    violence and aggression, 125–6
Roper, N., Logan, W. & Tierney, A., Model of
    Nursing (1980), 26

Safety, Health and Welfare at Work Act 1989,
    50–1
Safety, Health and Welfare at Work Act 2005,
    50, 51–68, 92
Safety, Health and Welfare at Work (General
    Applications) Regulations 1993, 62, 64
safety and health at work, 3, 4–5, 50–68
    fire, 55–7
    first aid, 62–4
    infection control, 57–62

legislation, 50–1
manual handling, 64–6
risk assessment, hazards and risks, 52–3
risk factors, 66–7
safety statement, 51, 53
work environment, 53–5
safety needs, 33–4
safety signs, 55
safety statements, 51, 53
St Christopher's Hospice, London, 135
St John Ambulance Brigade, 62–3
St Vincent de Paul, 114
Saunders, Dame Cecily, 133, 135
schizophrenia, 156–8
Scrutton, S., 14
self-esteem, promoting, 18–20
Senior Citizens Parliament, 102
Senior Help Line, 114
senses, diminishing, 33
sensitive procedures, 17–18
separation
    challenging behaviour, 122
service-user factors
    challenging behaviour, 118
sexual health, 67
sexuality, expressing, 44–5
sharps, disposal of, 61–2
shelter, 33
sign language, 74–5
skills audit, 82–5
skin, care of, 98. see also pressure sores
sleep, 45
smell, diminished sense of, 33
smoking, 67
social factors
    challenging behaviour, 120
social needs, 43–4
social relationships, 12–13
source isolation, 60–1
spiritual needs, 35, 77–8
Spokes, K. et al., 119
staff, and challenging behaviour, 118–19,
    125, 130–1
STIs, 67

stoma, management of, 38
stress, 67
stroke, 106–7
Stuart, G.W. and Laria, M.T., 154, 155, 158
support care, 4
  care needs, 21–2
  human growth and development, 22–5
  reflective practice, 27–31
symptom management (palliative care),
    143–5

Taylor and Navaco, 121–2
teeth, cleaning, 41–2
telephone, 72
terminal care, 145–7
  cultural considerations, 148
  last offices, 147–8
Terms of Employment (Information) Act
    1994, 92
The Irish Longitudinal Study on Ageing
    (TILDA), 102
therapeutic communication, 76–8
Total Parenteral Nutrition (TPN), 36
touch
  and communication, 74
  failing sense of, 33
  need for, 44–5
Travelling community, 148
treatment-related factors
  challenging behaviour, 122
Trinity College Dublin (TCD), 102
Trust in Care Policy, 125

urinary drainage, assisted, 37
urinary incontinence, 38–9
urinary system, ageing, 99

verbal communication, 71
violence, management of, 125–6
vision, impaired, 107–8
vulnerable clients, 14–16, 125

waste disposal, 61–2
Waterlow, Braden and Norton, 48
wellness, promoting, 14
Wittington, 124
women, and privacy, 18
Worden, J.W., 149
work experience, 3, 5, 80–95
  aim of, 85
  employment opportunities, 81–2
  globalisation and demographics, 80–1
  interview skills, 91–2
  setting goals, 85–6
  skills audit, 82–5
work presentation
  CV and application forms, 86–91
Working Group (DOHC, 2001), 2
World Health Organisation (WHO), 135,
    144, 151, 152–3
writing, 73